Unicorns Grayscale

An Adult Coloring Book

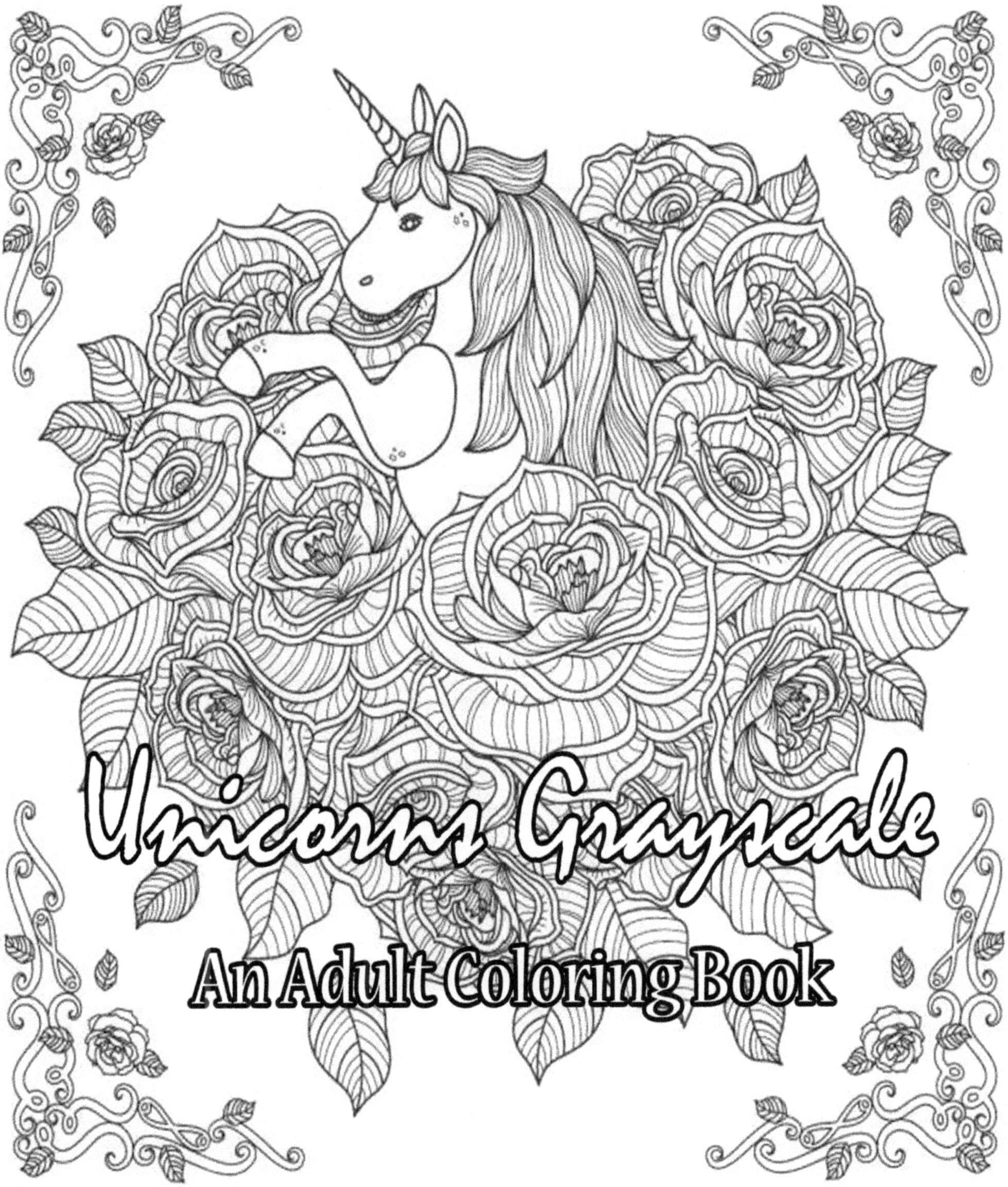

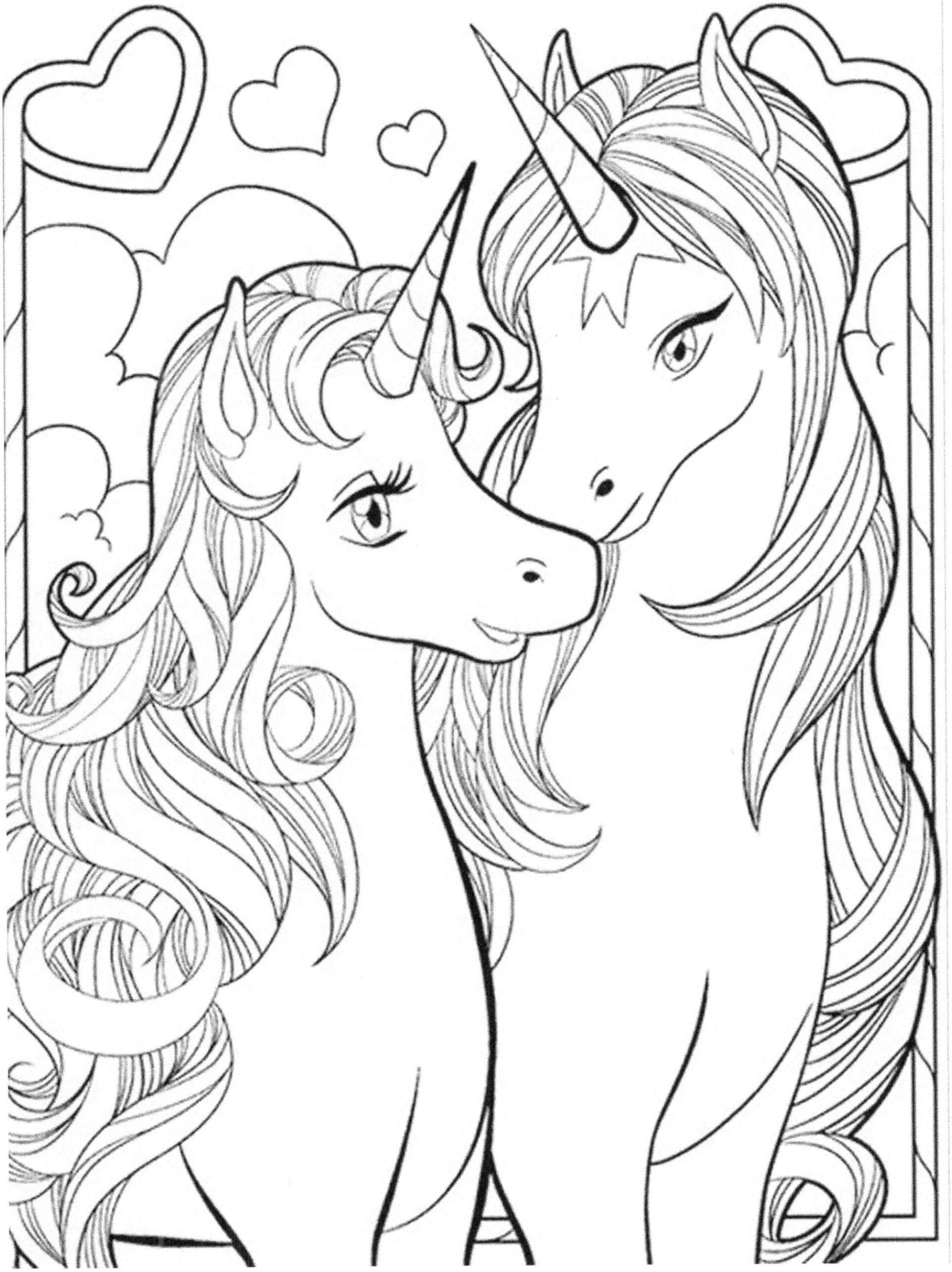

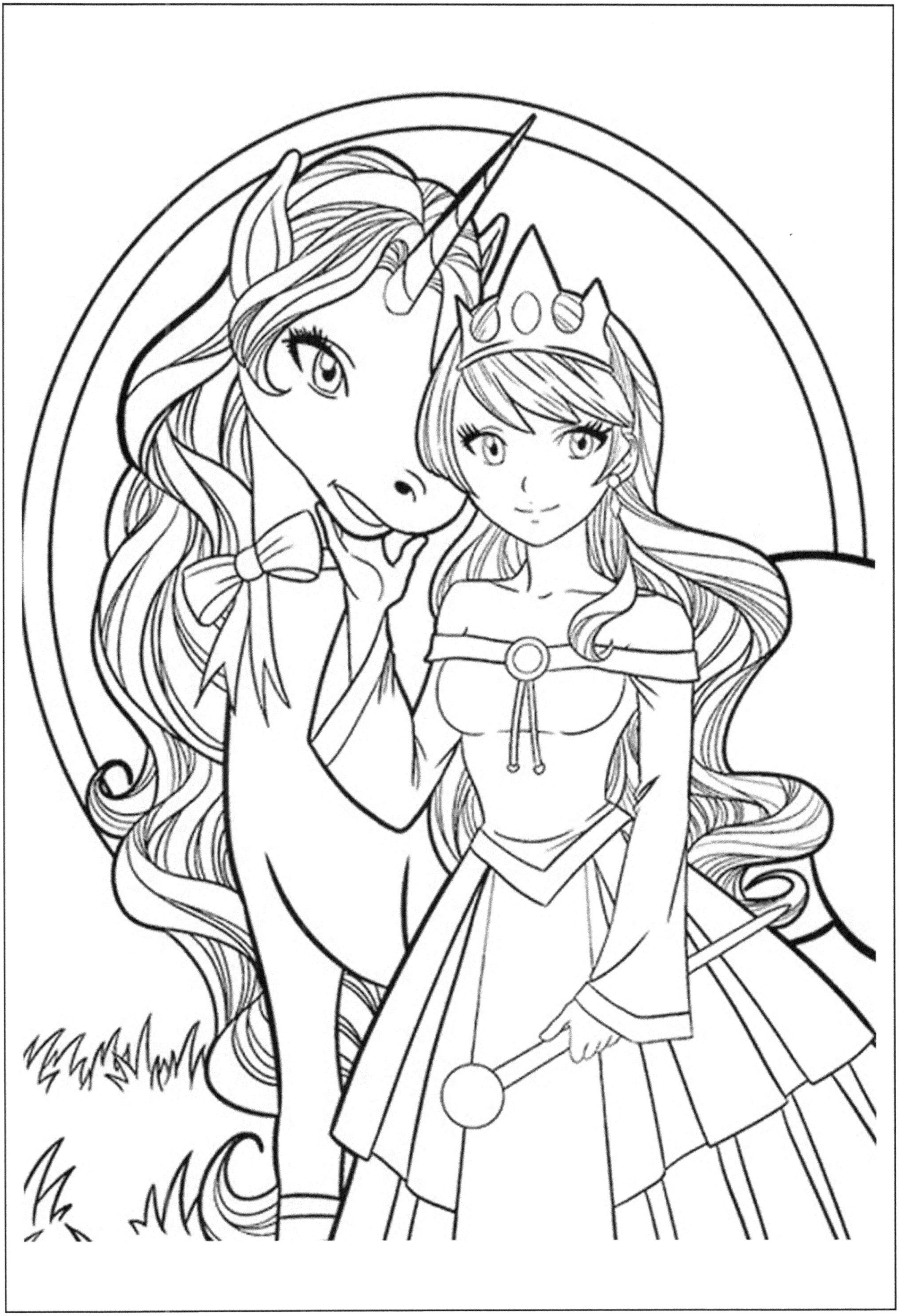

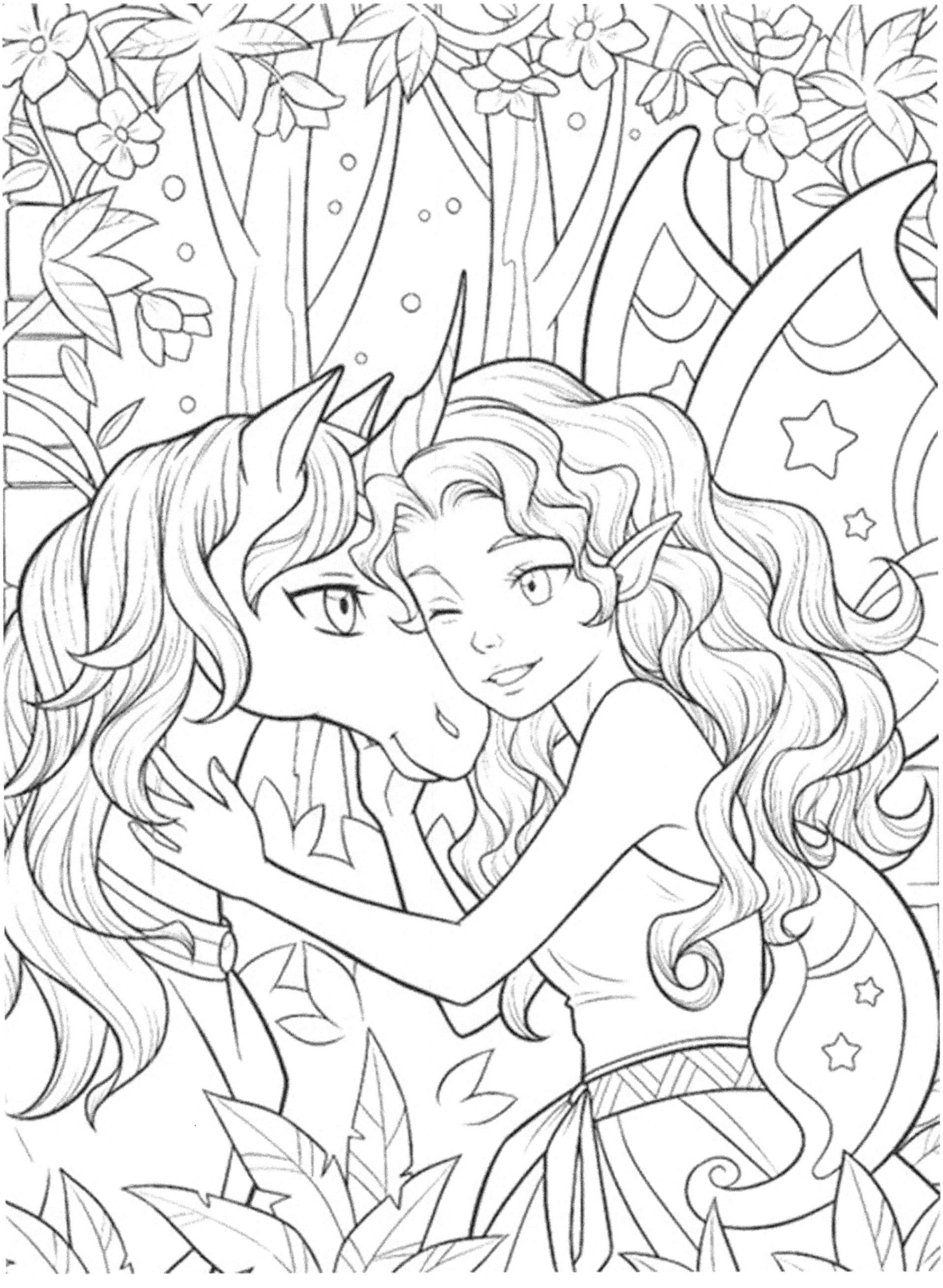

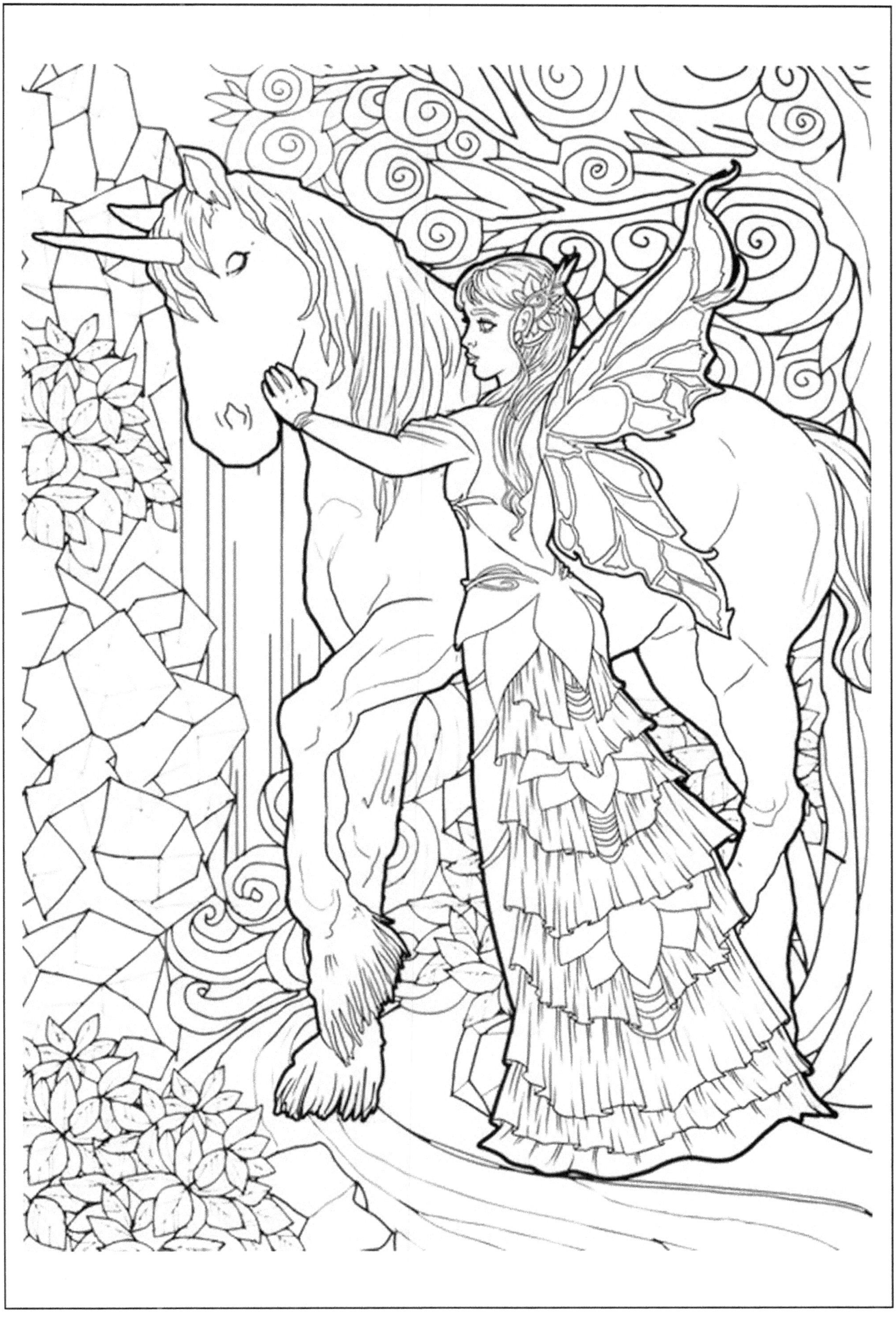

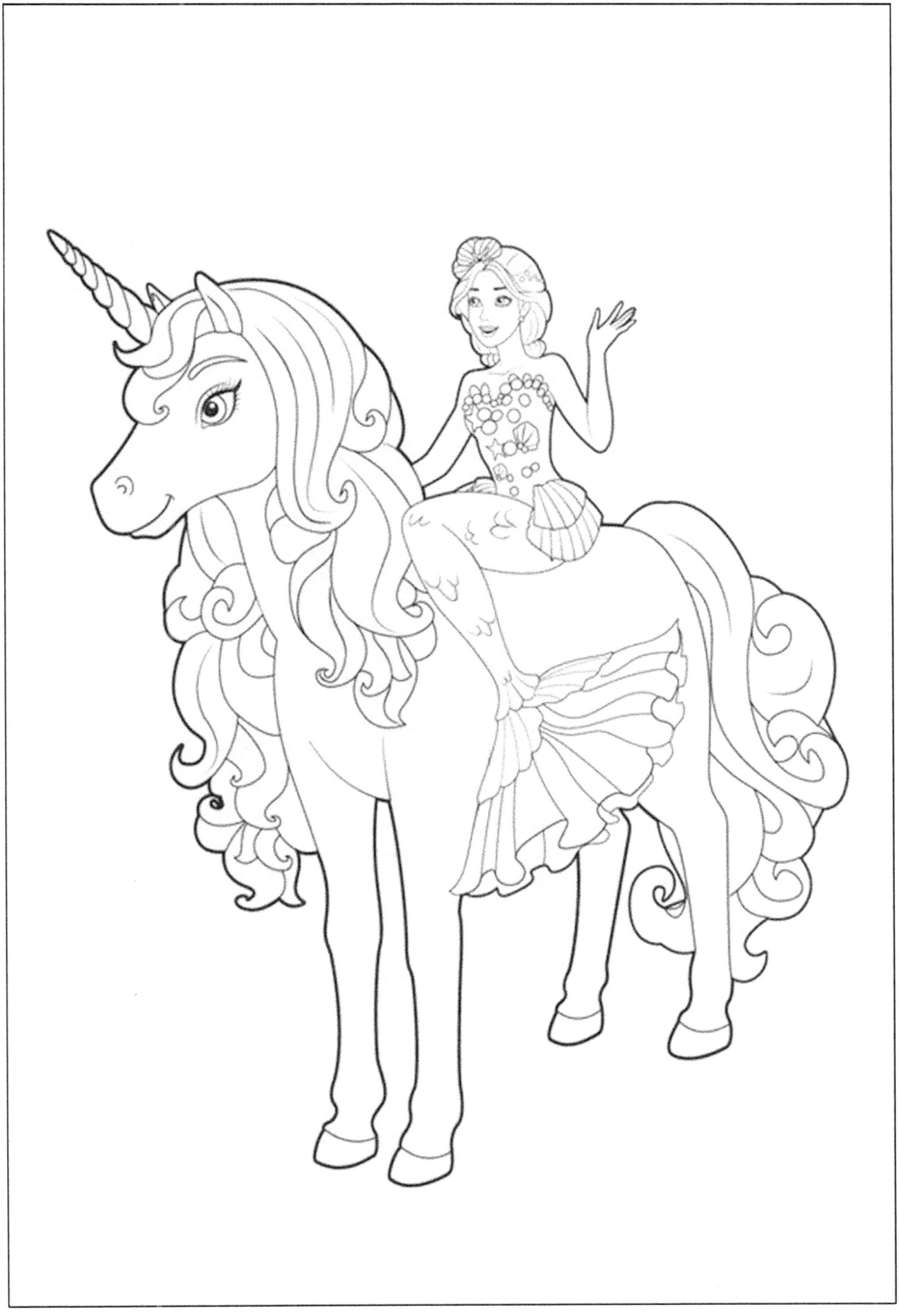

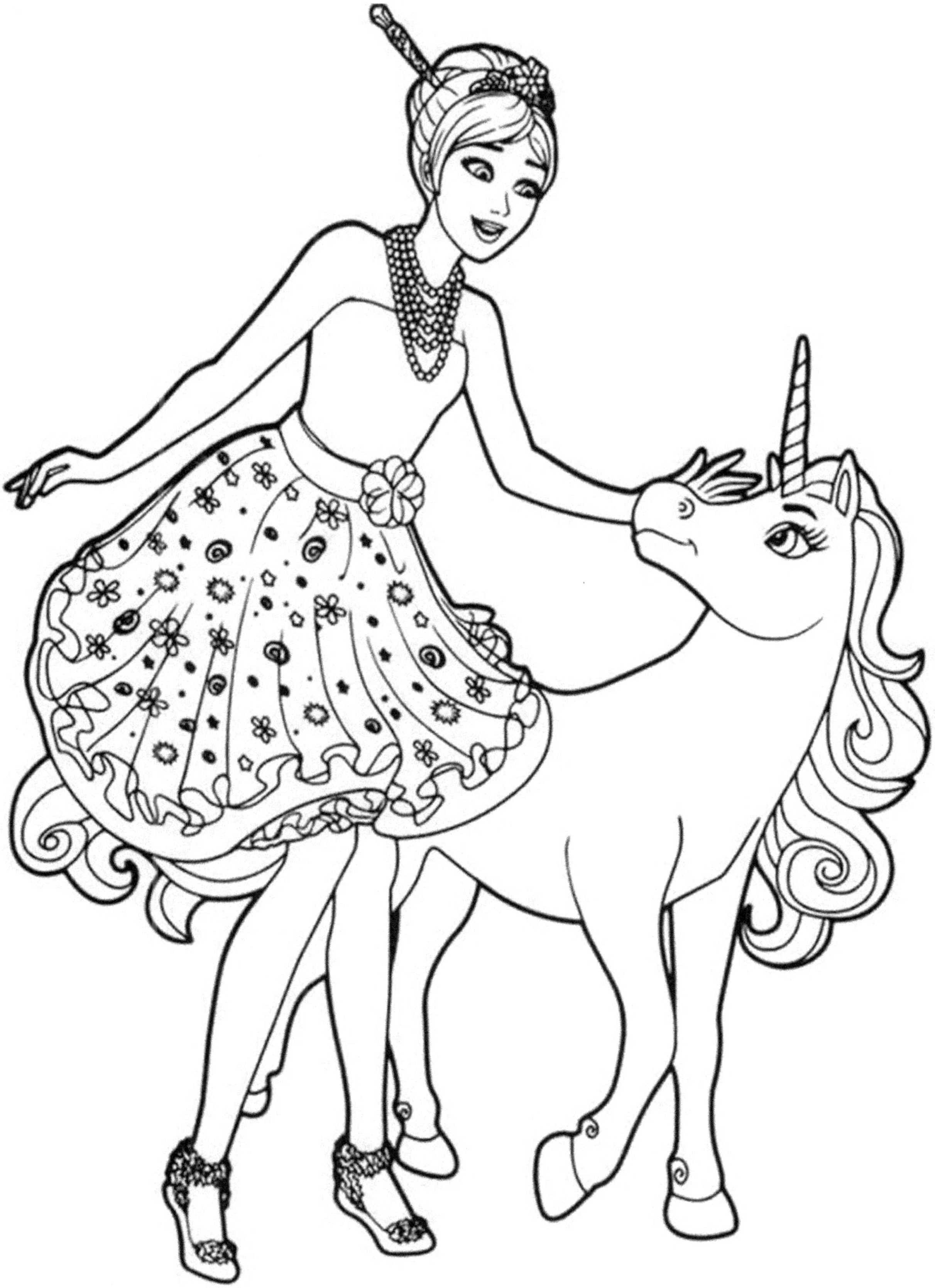

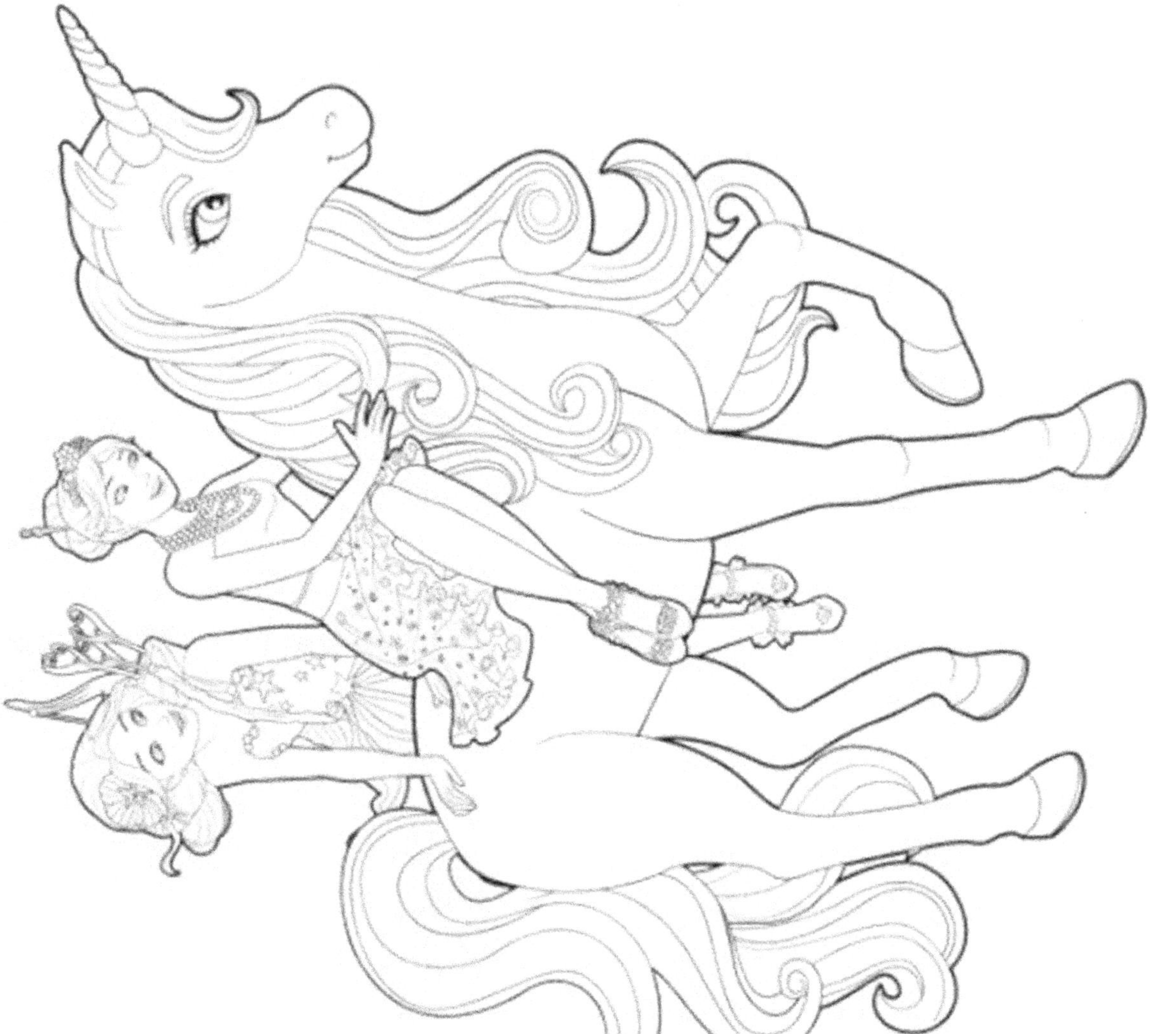

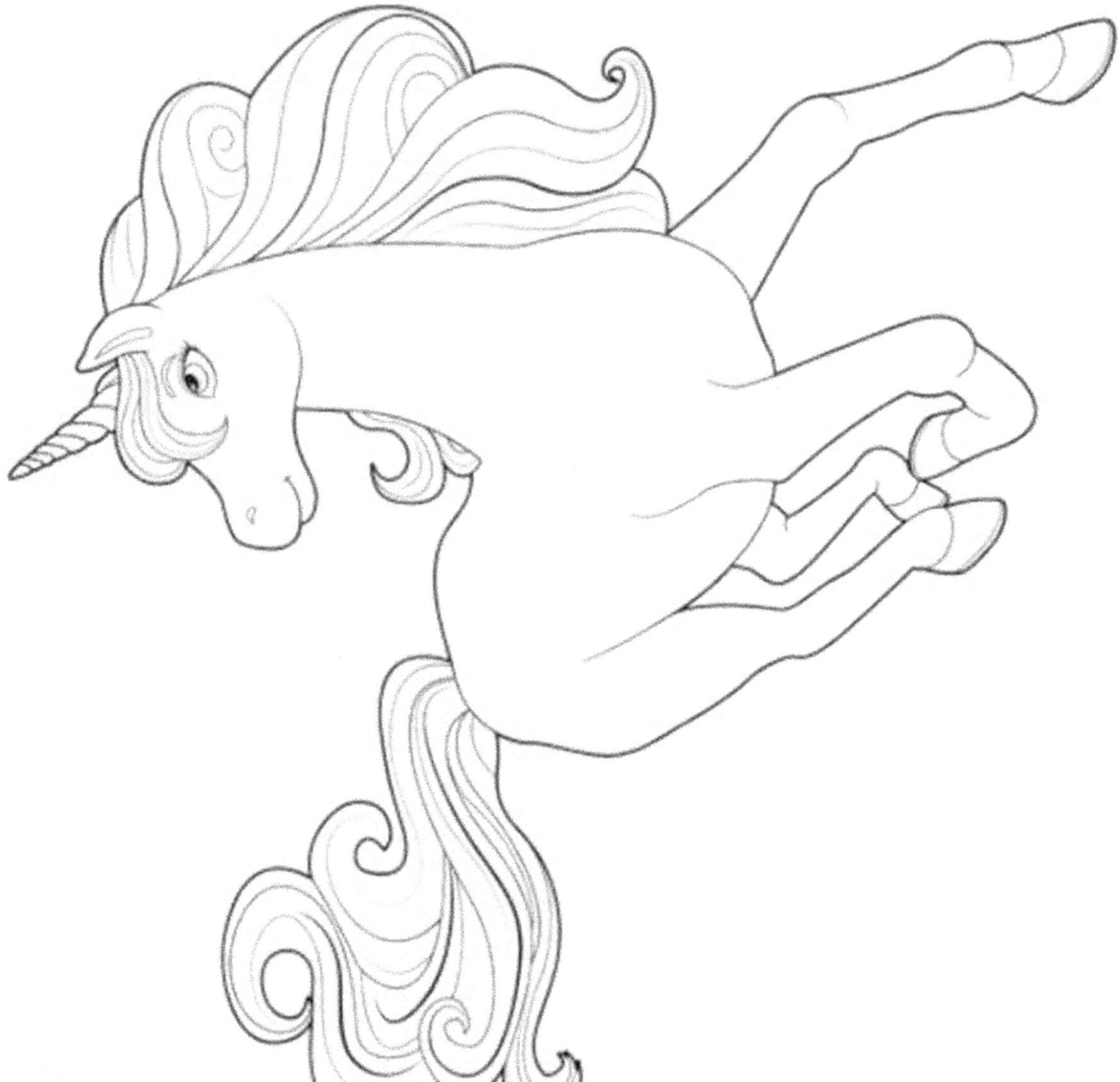

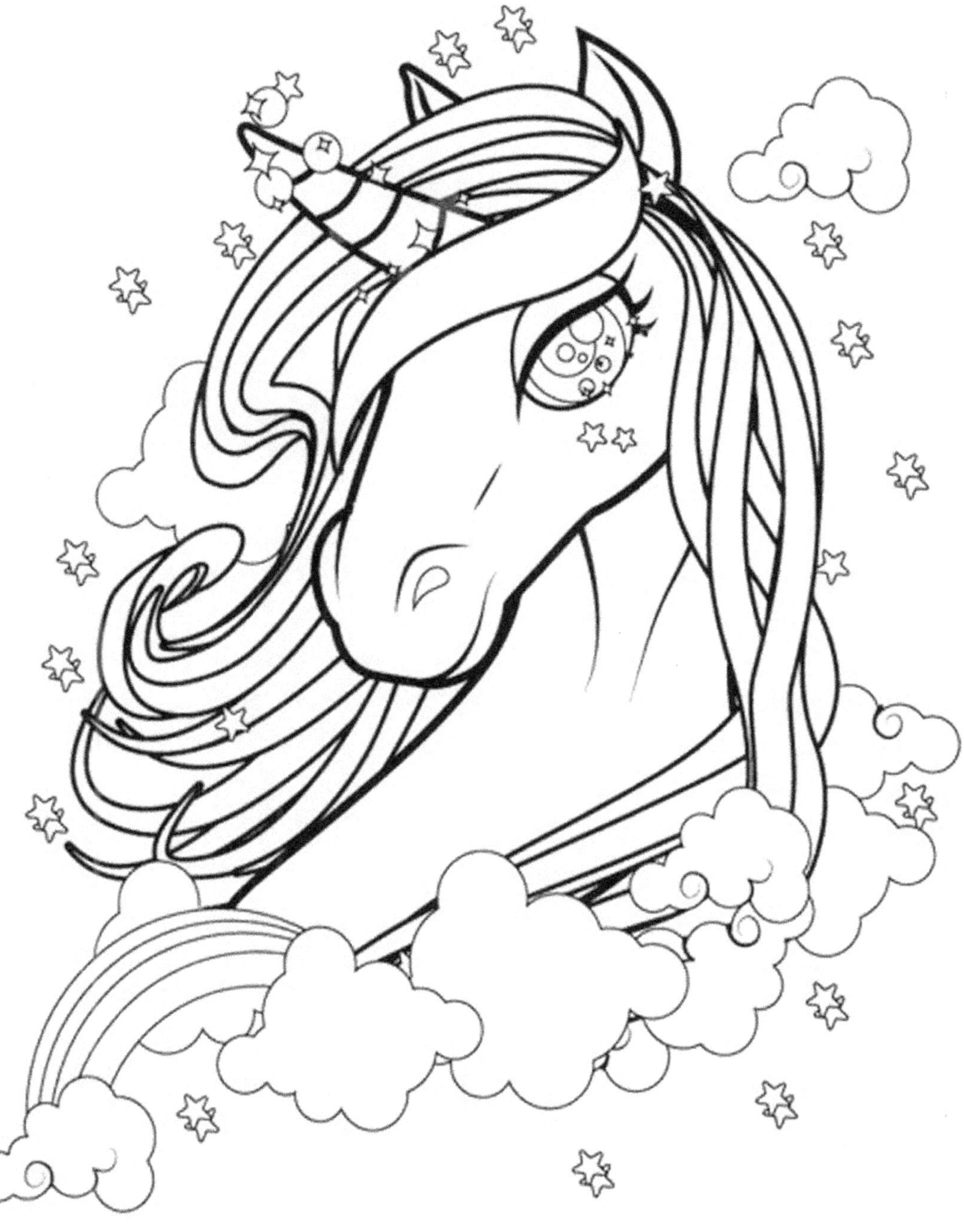

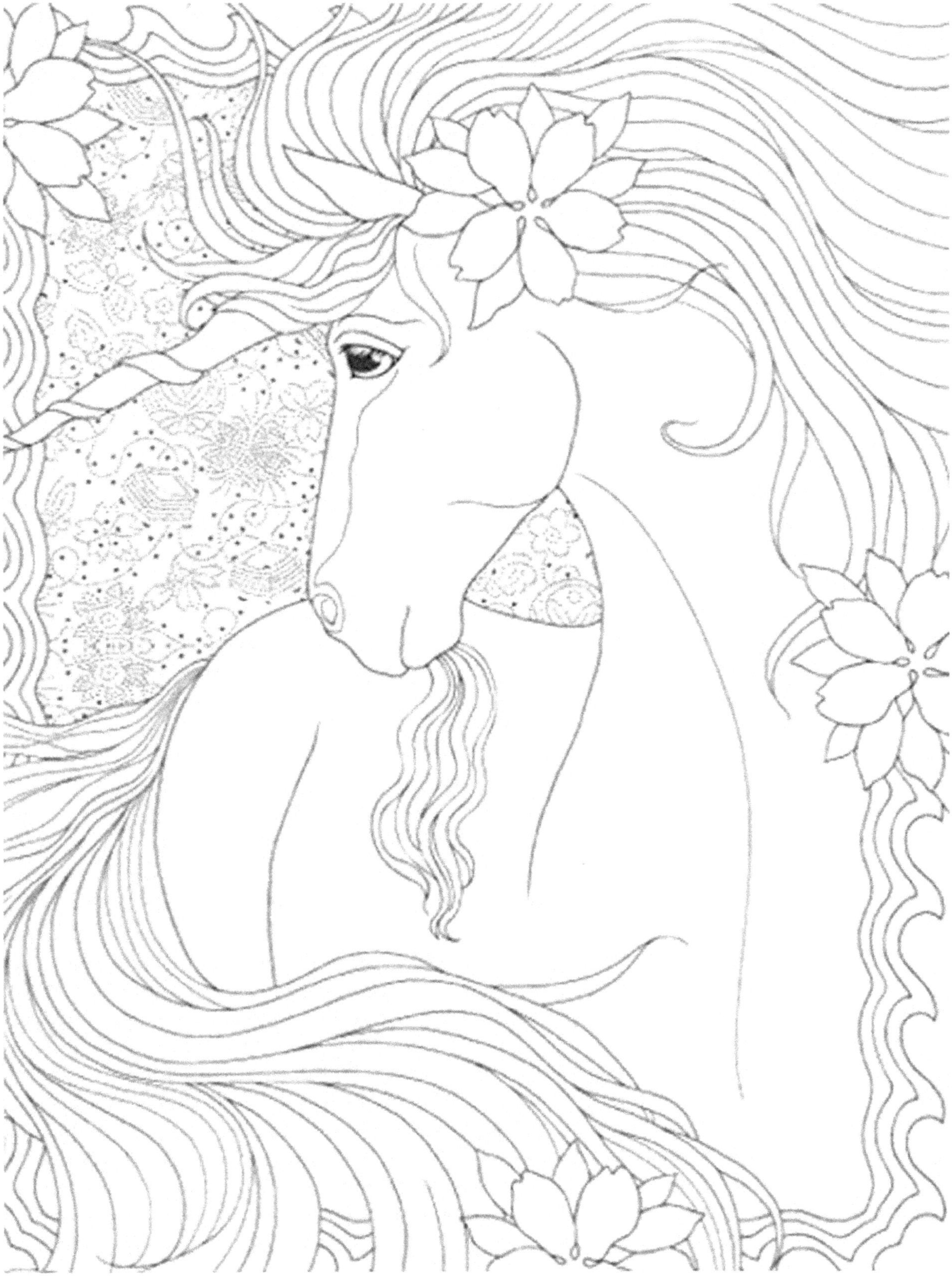

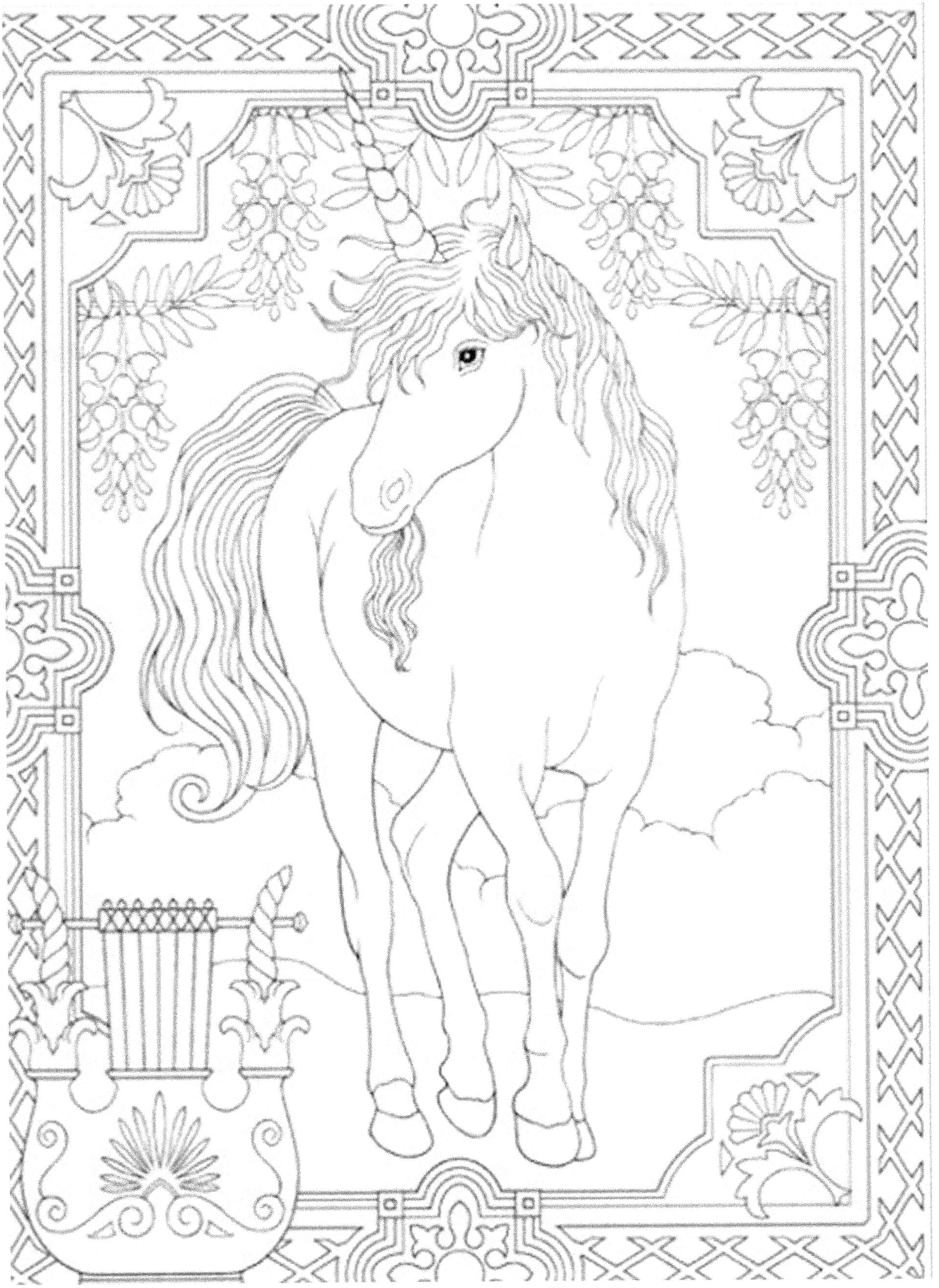

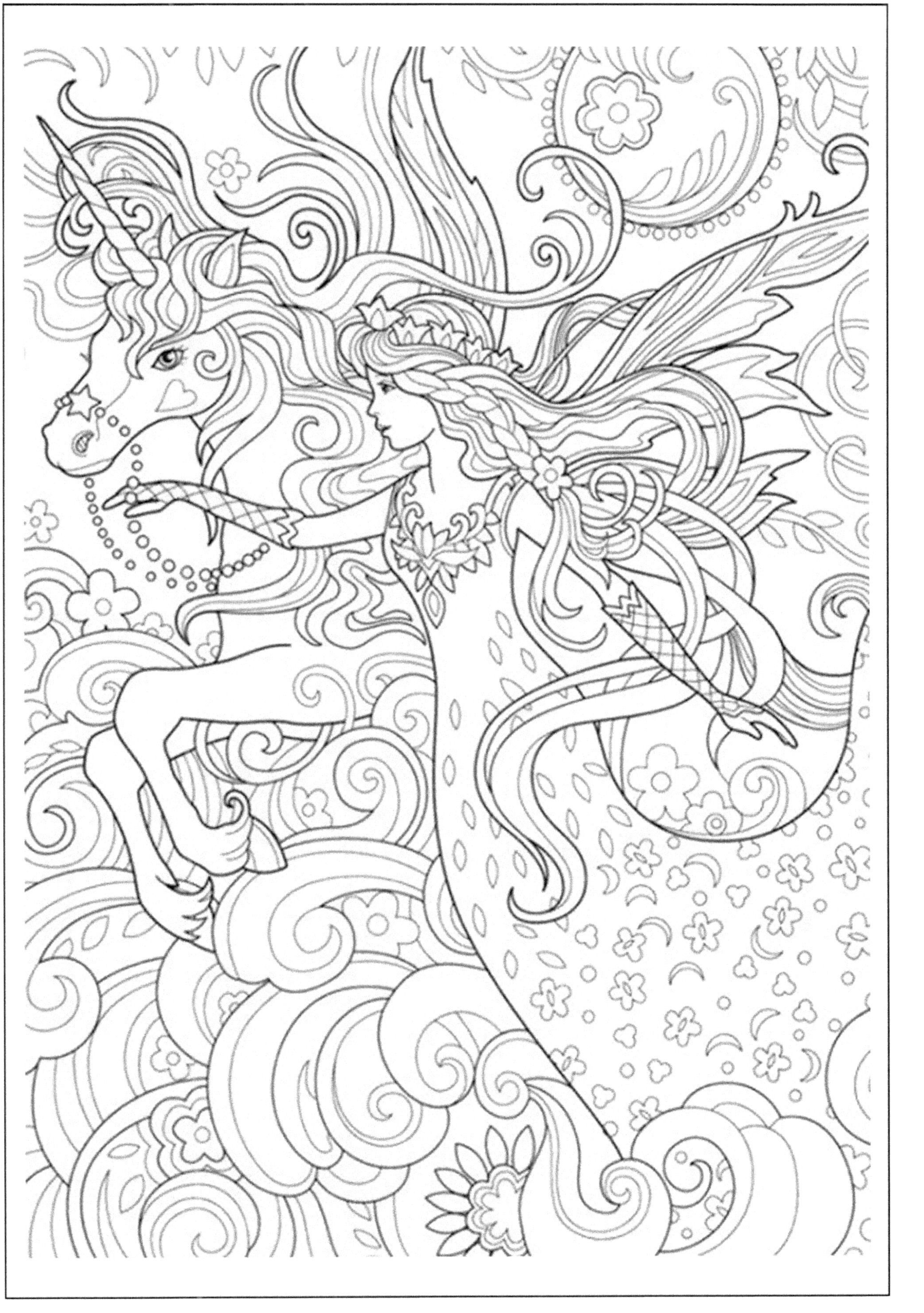

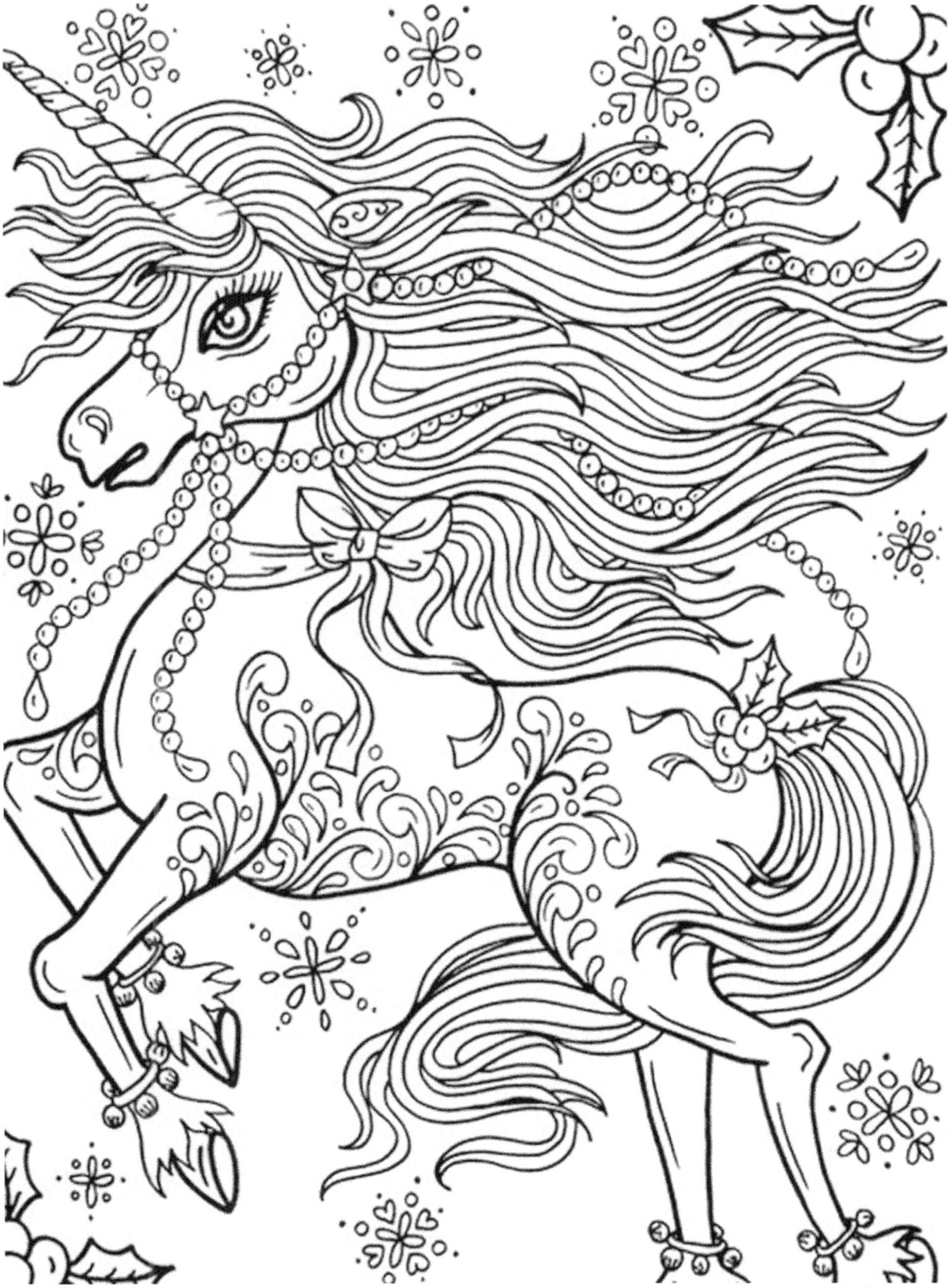

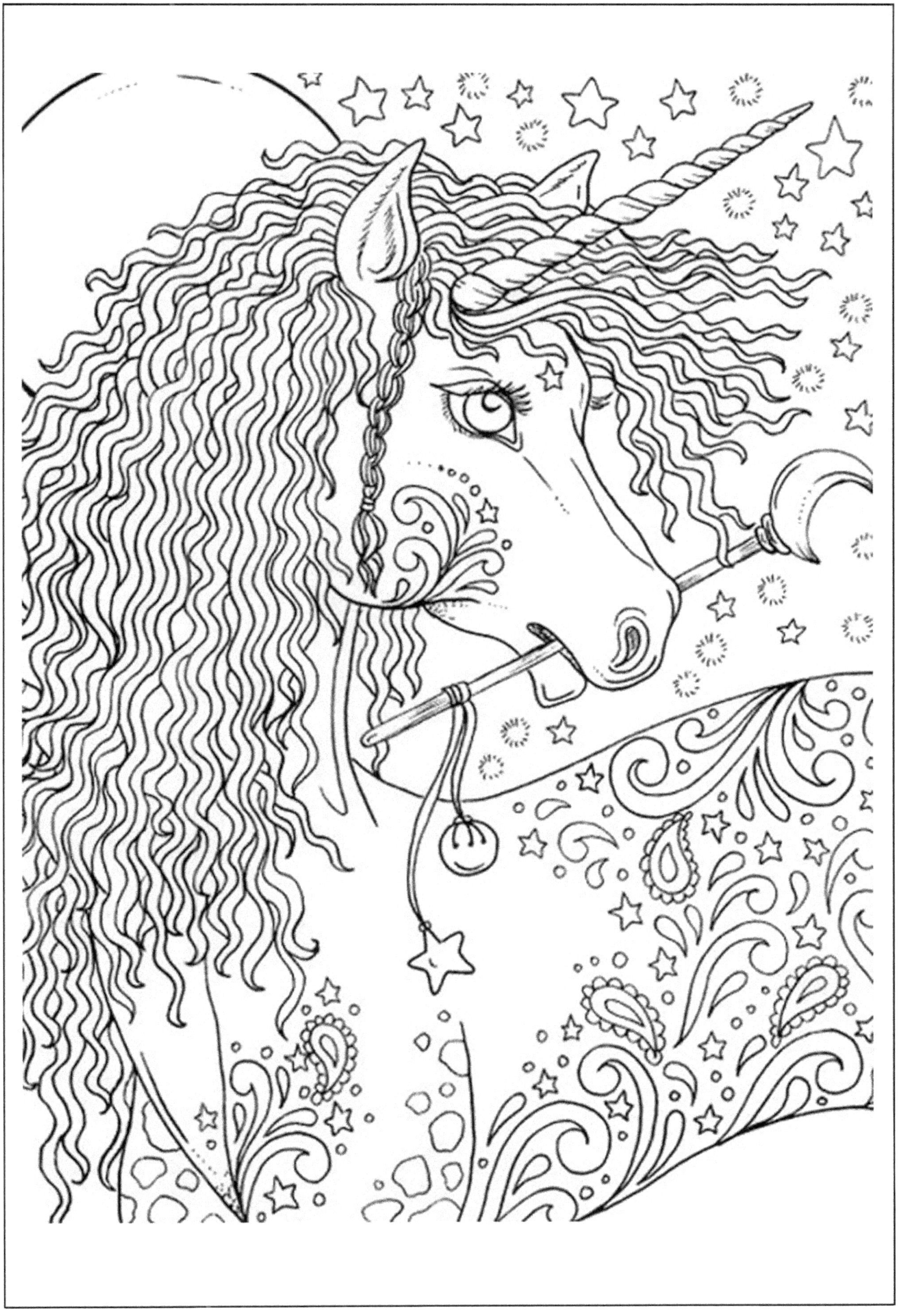

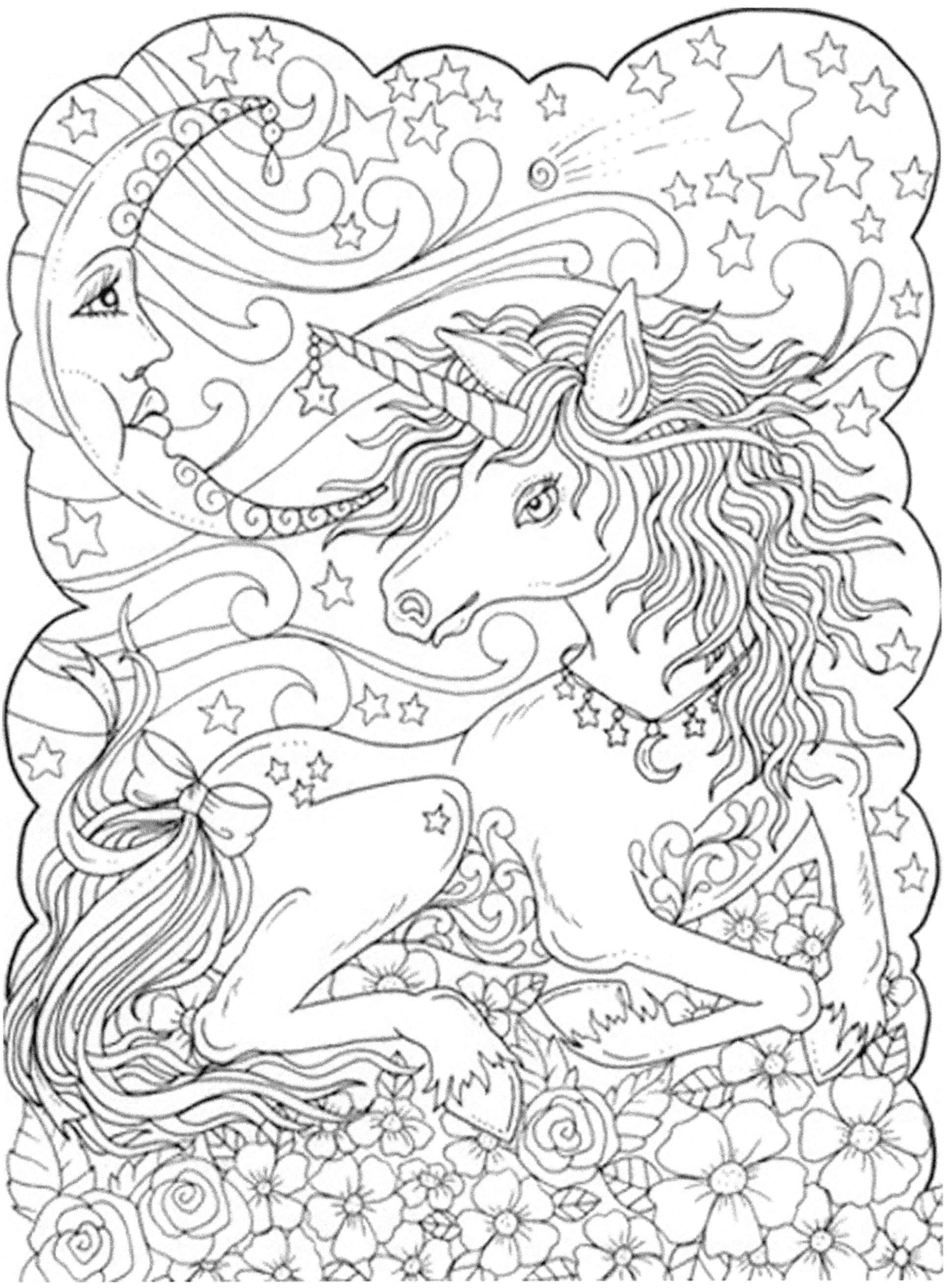

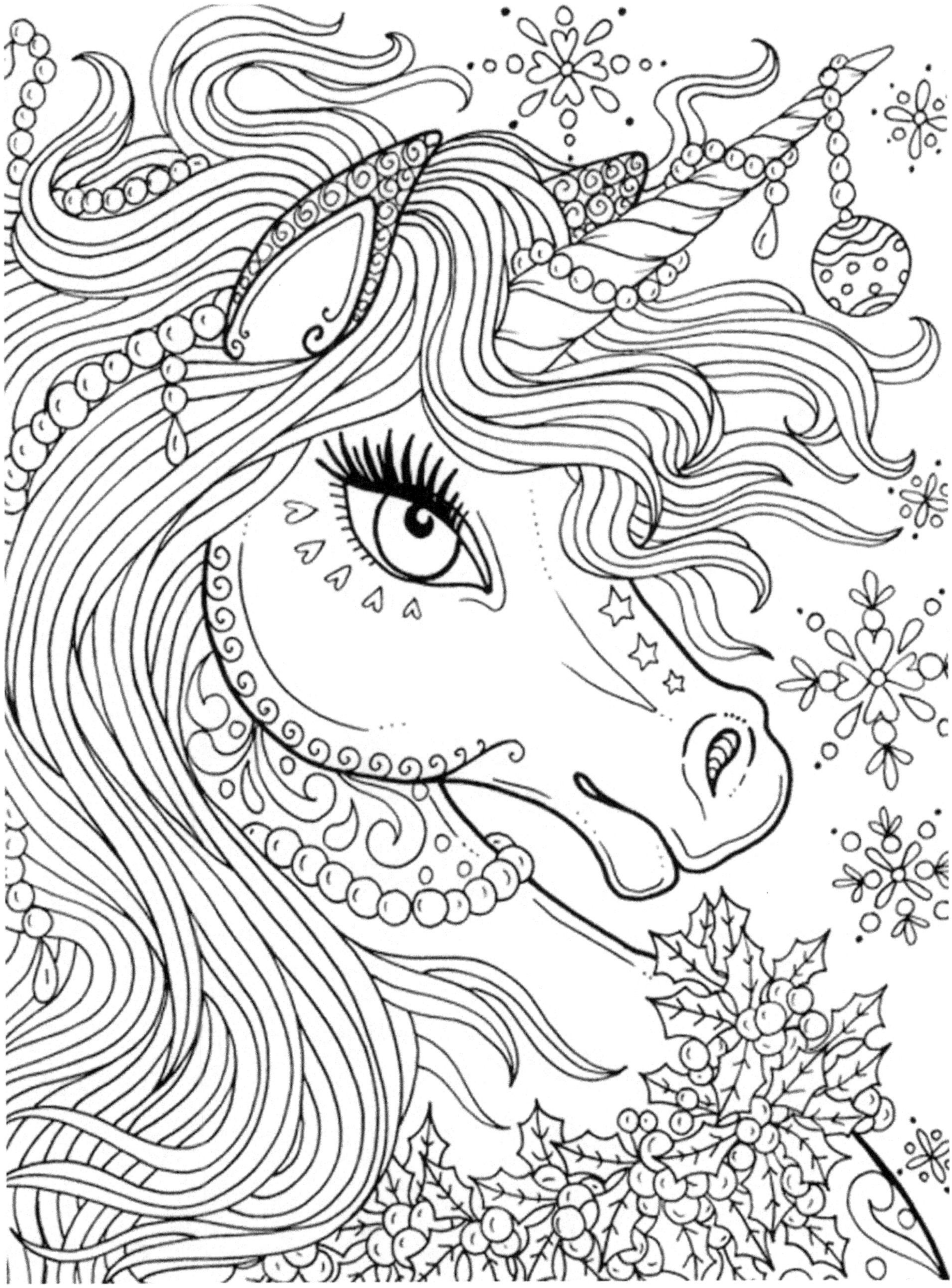

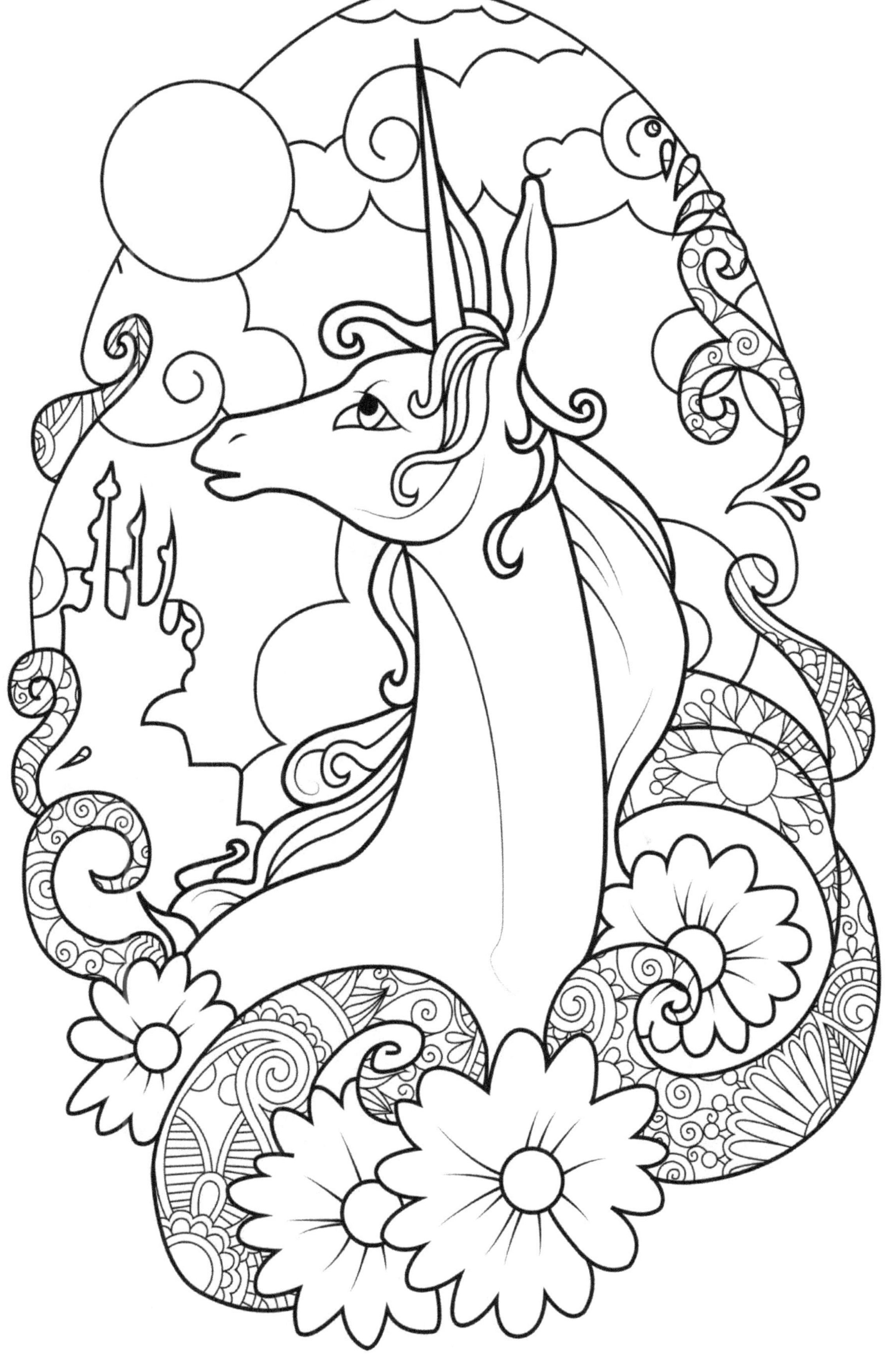

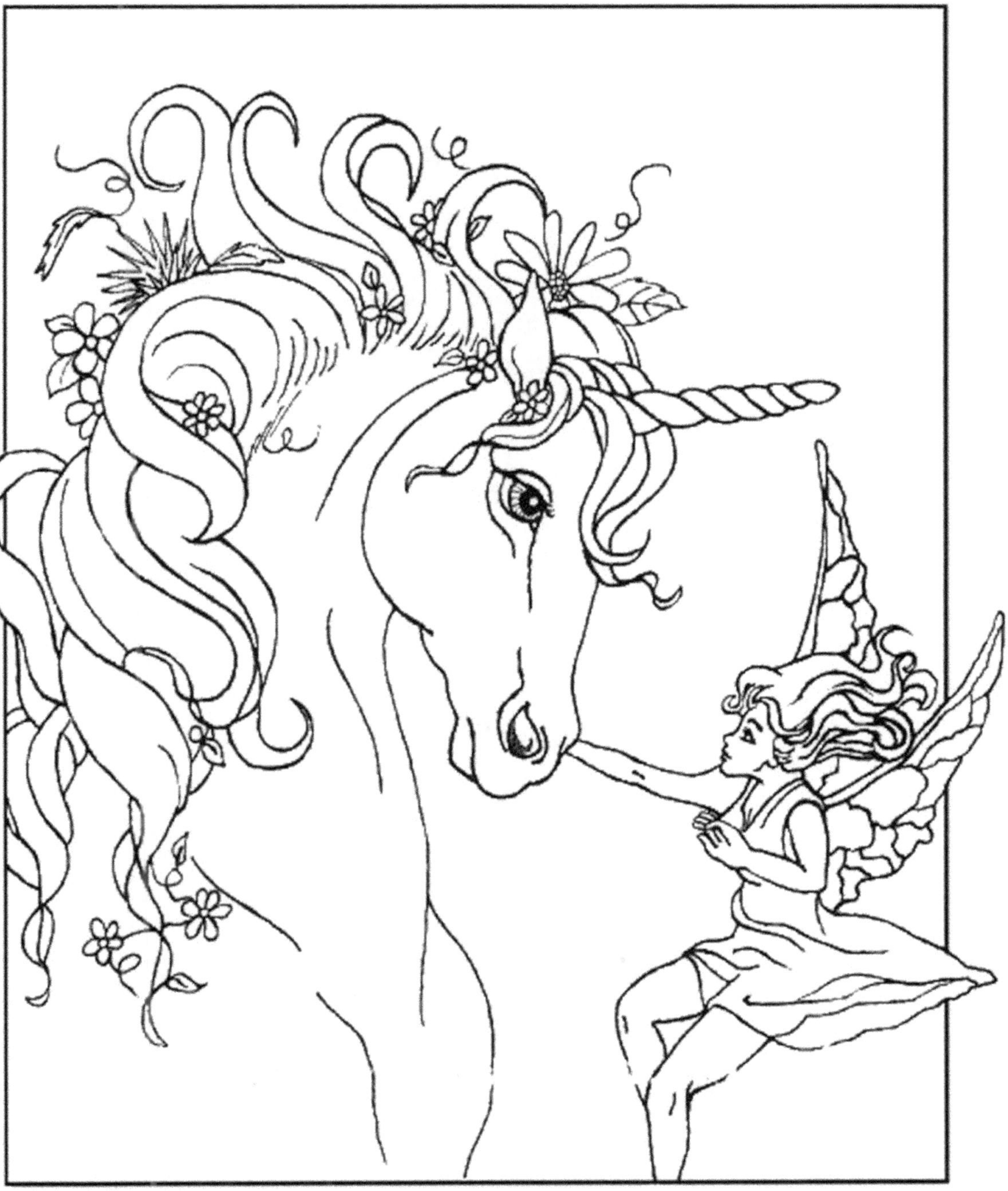

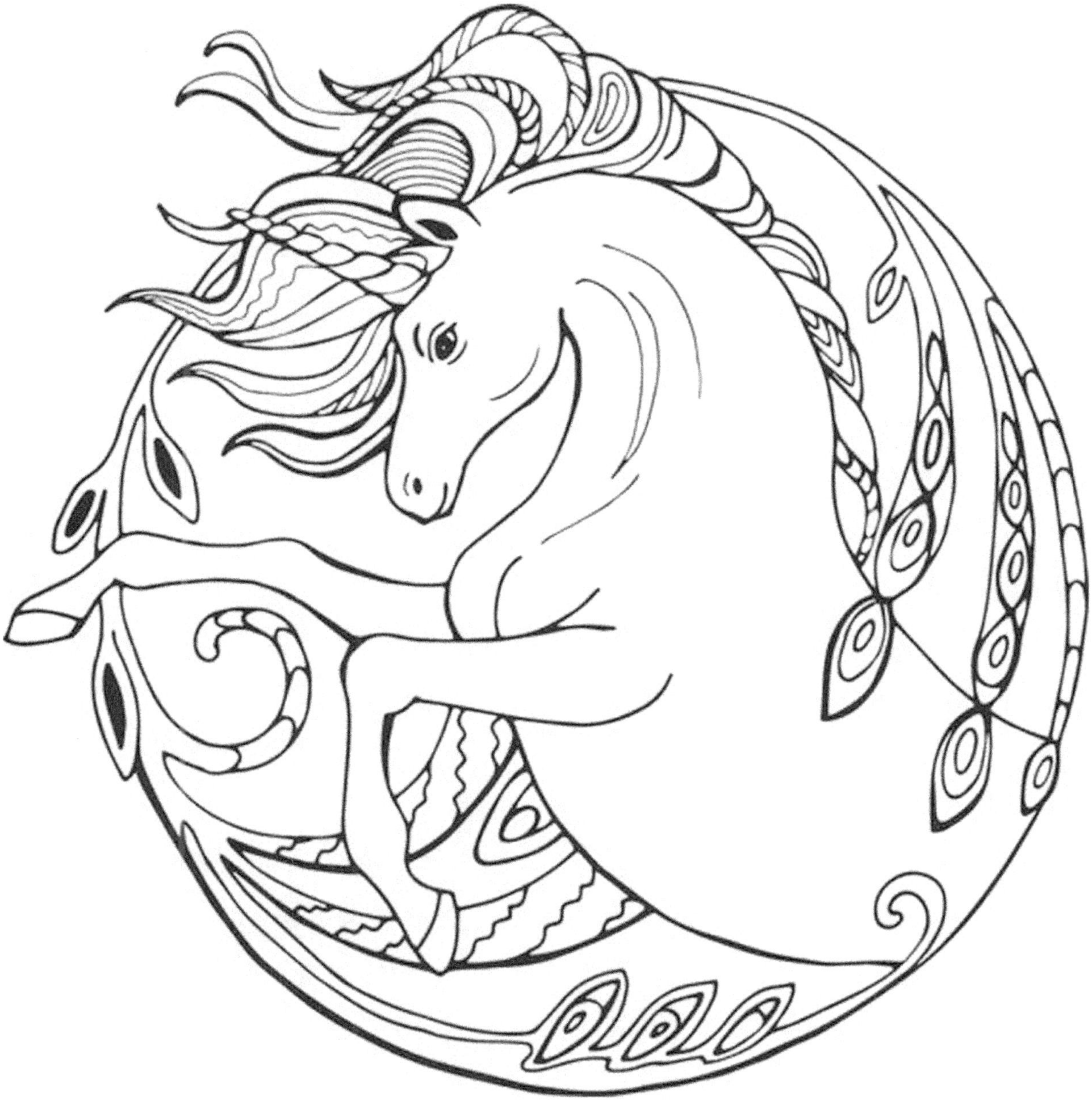

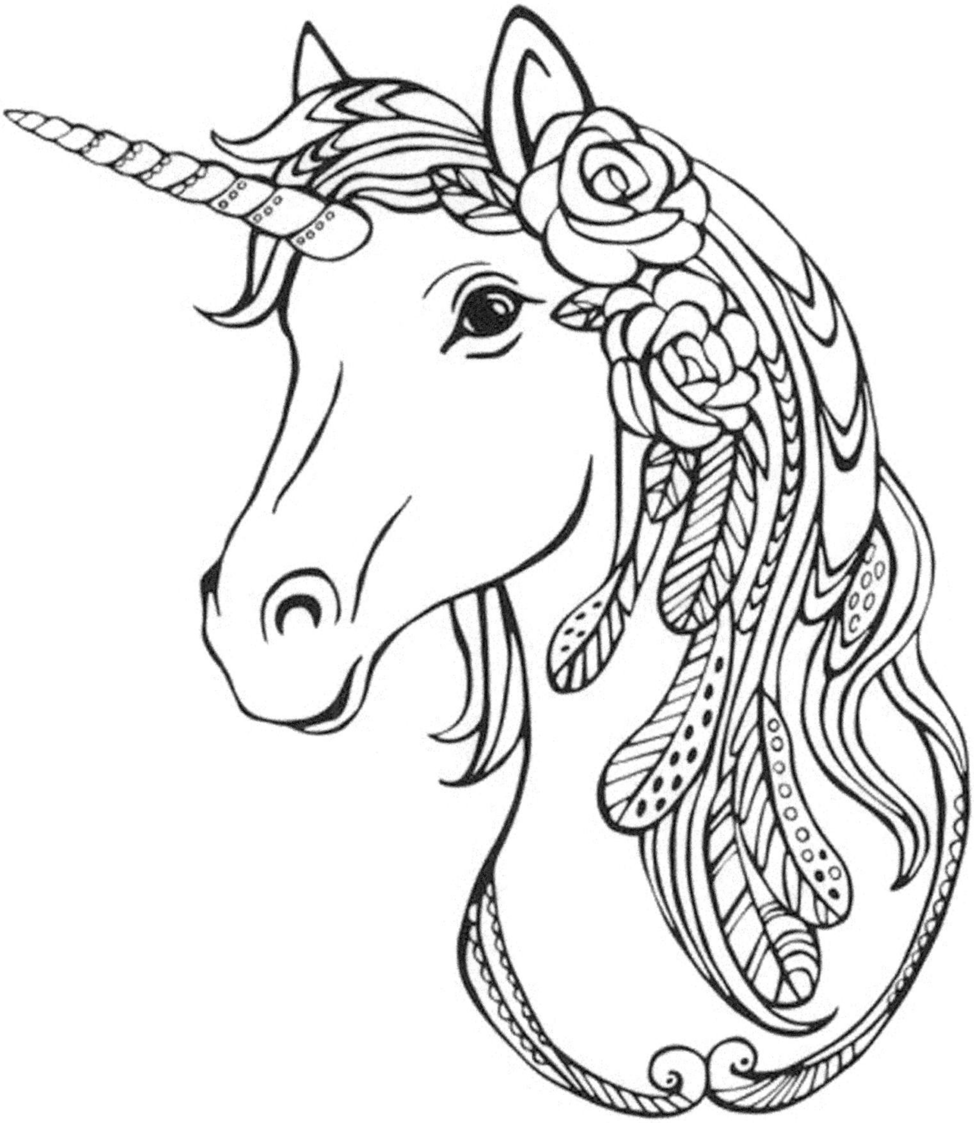

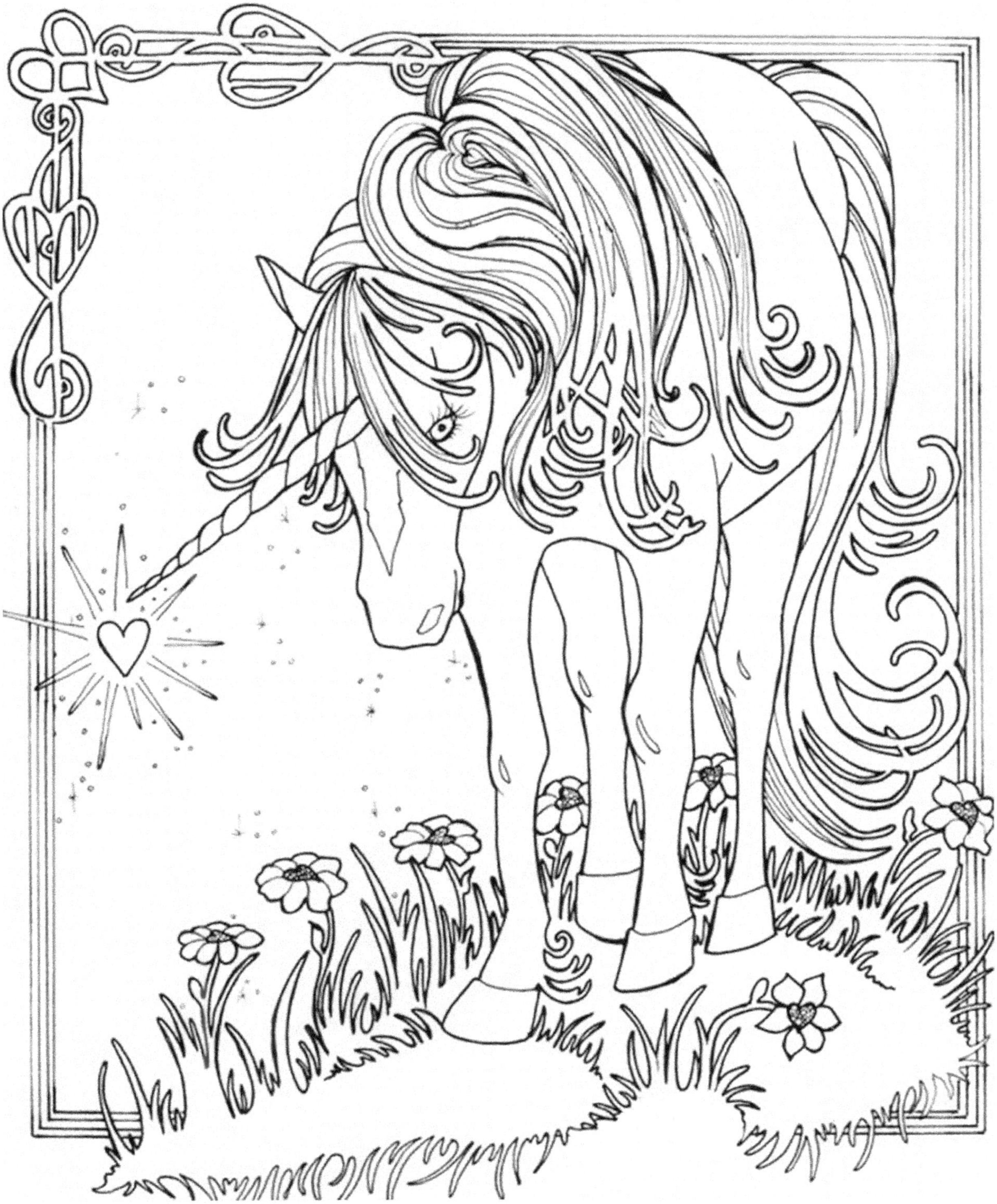

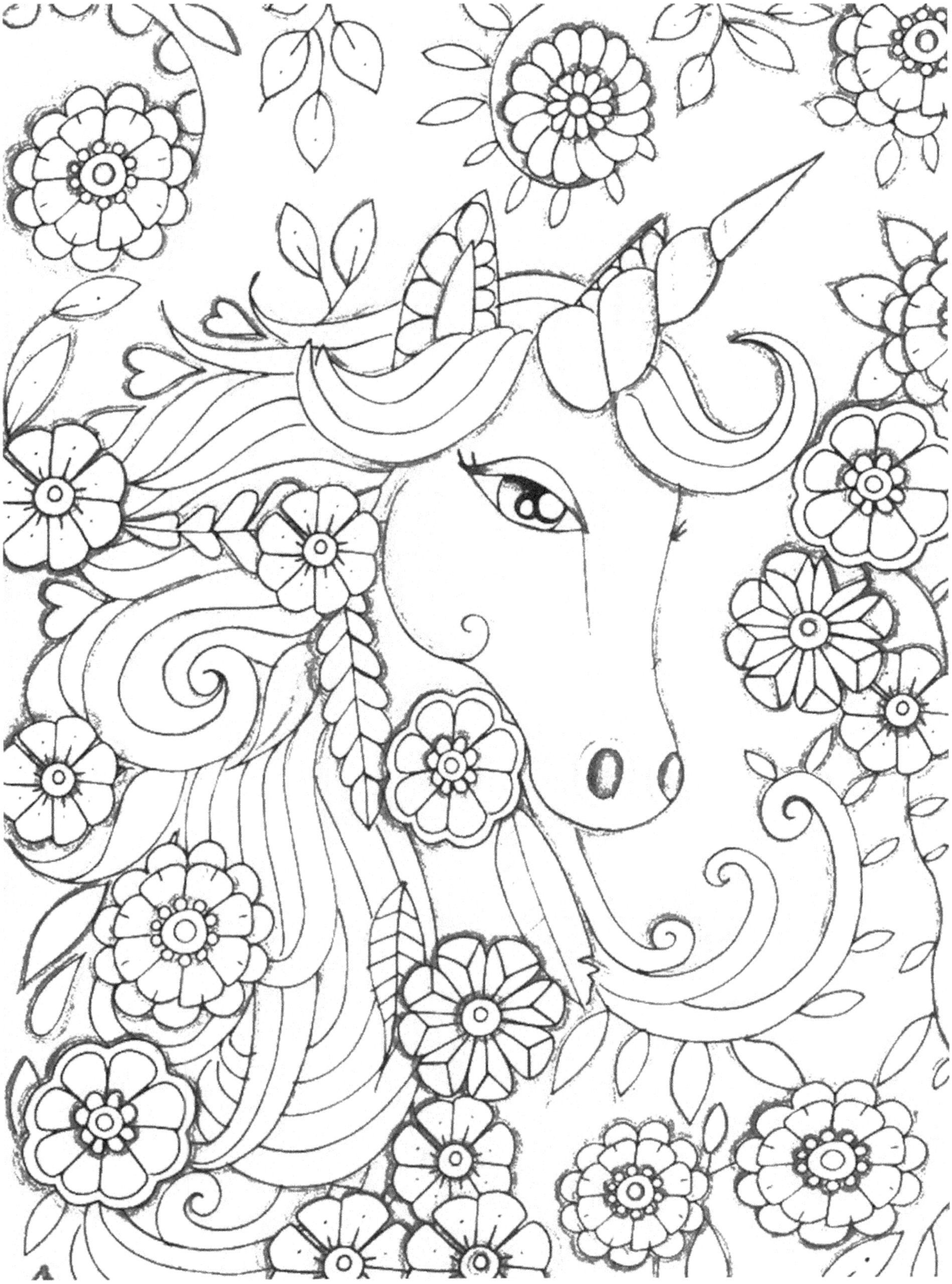

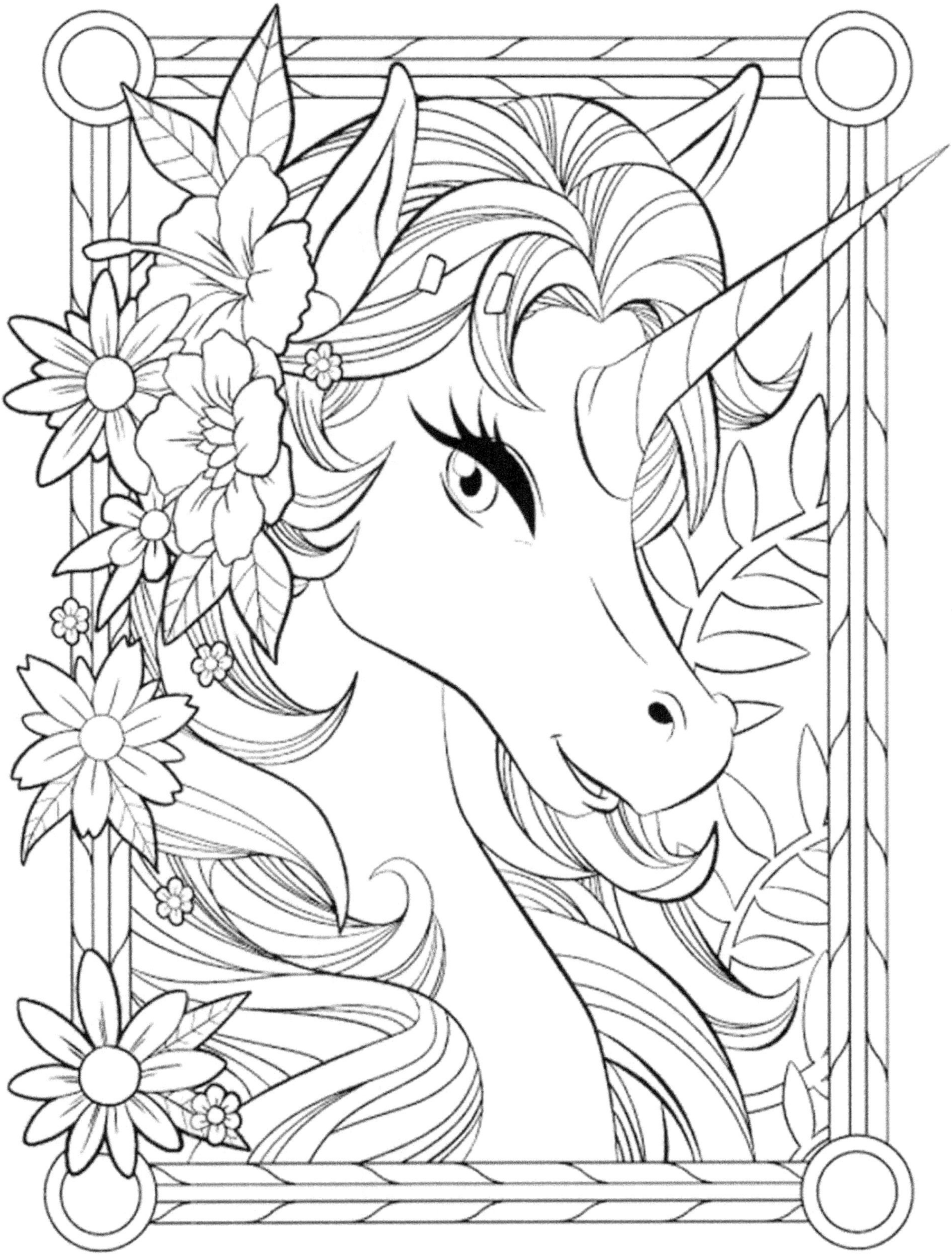

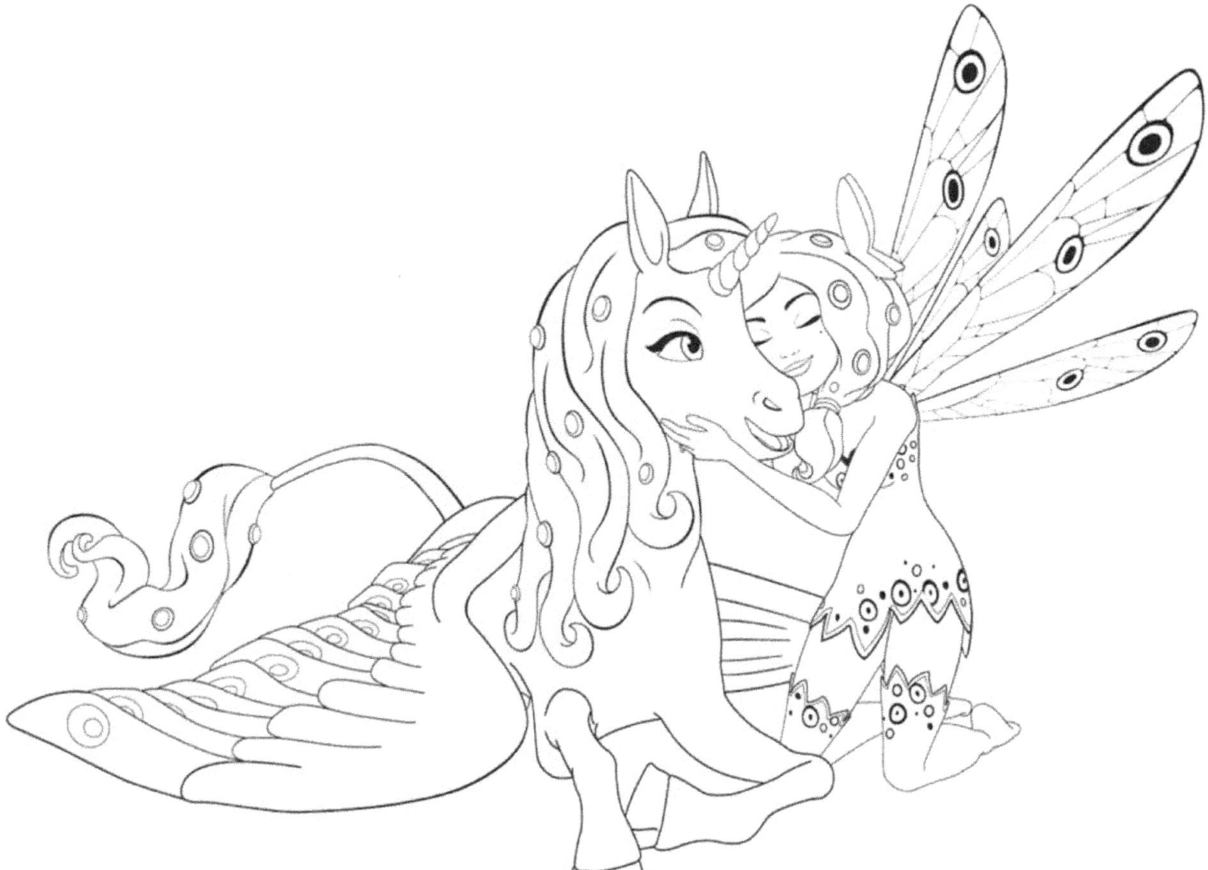

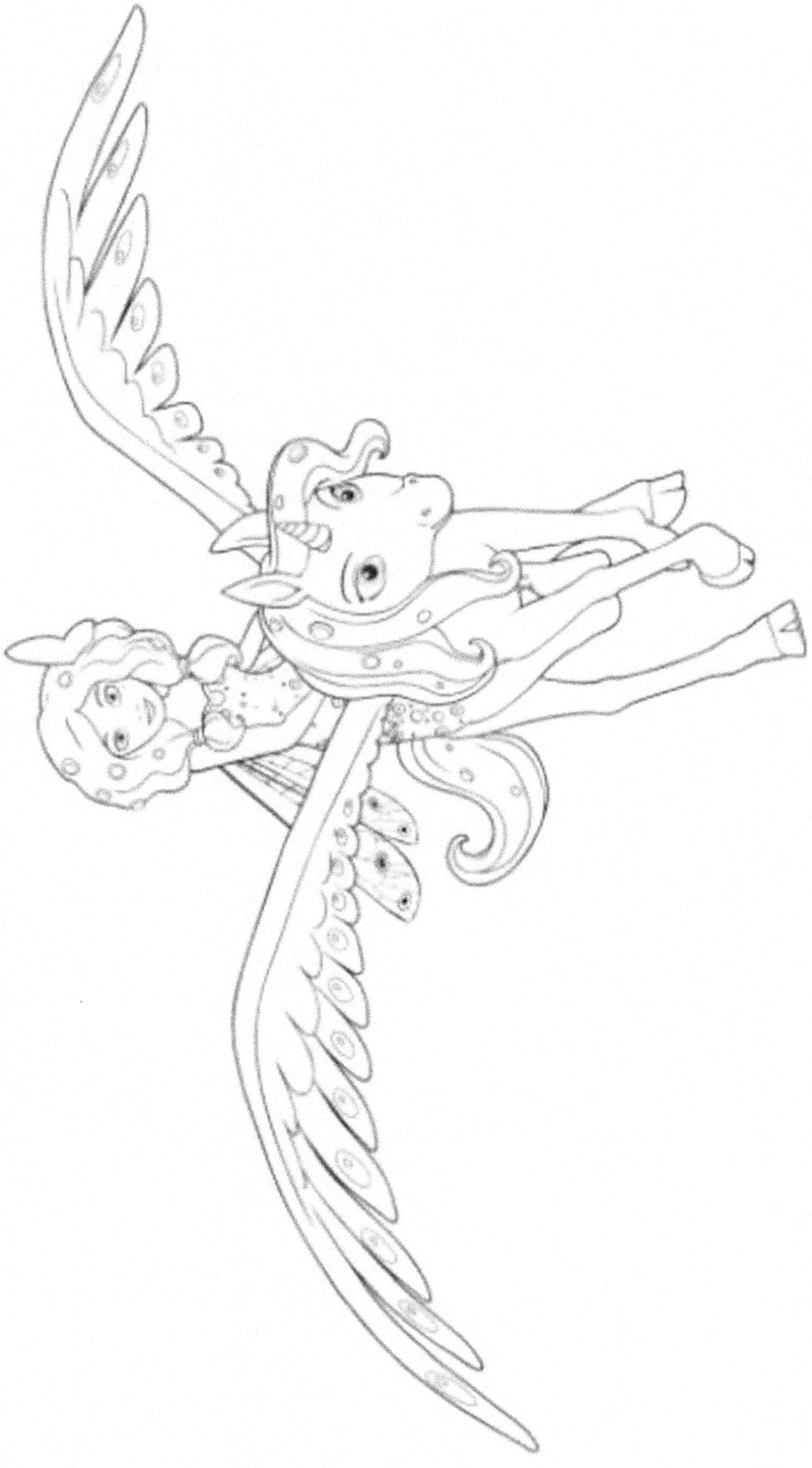

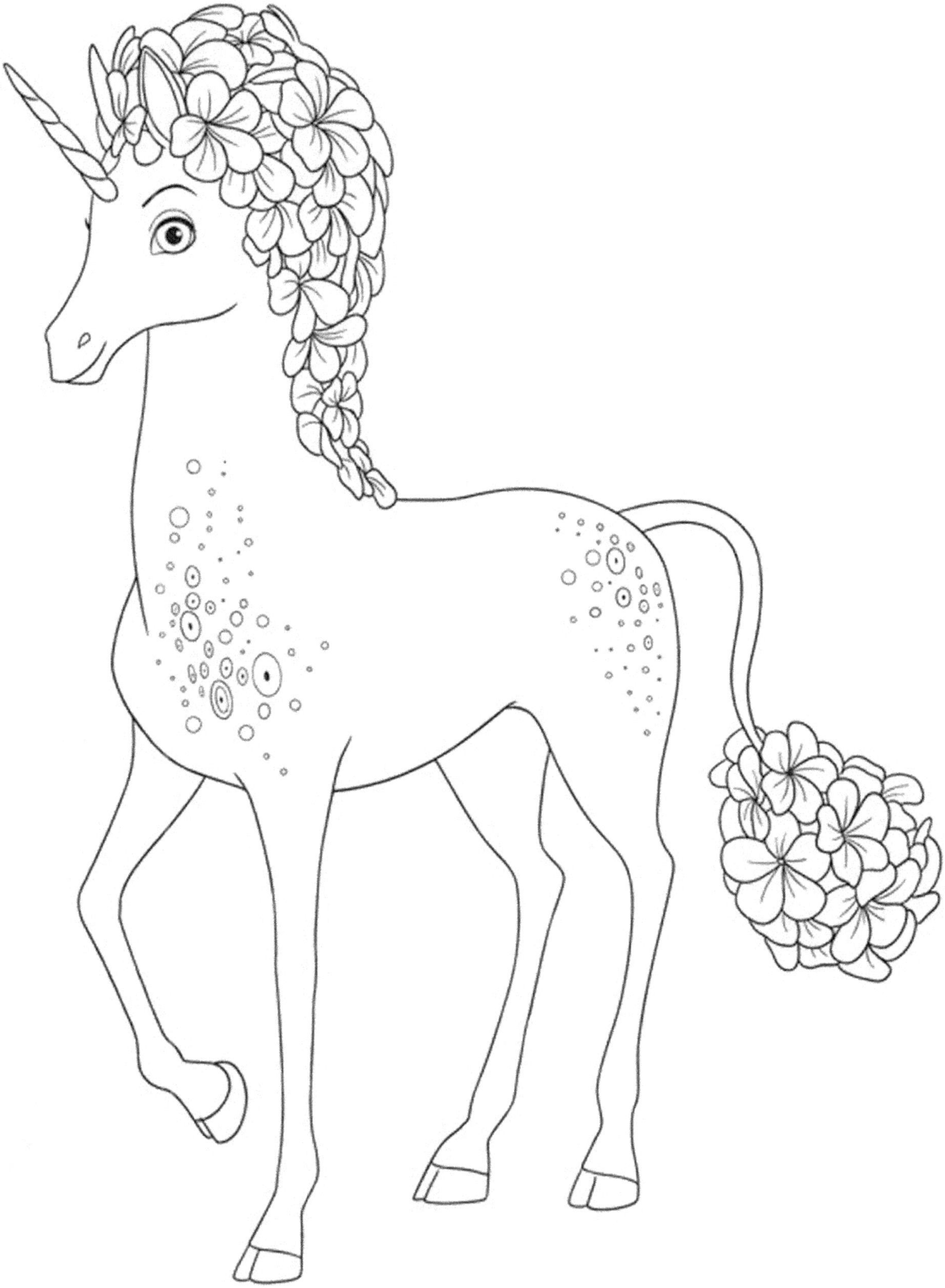

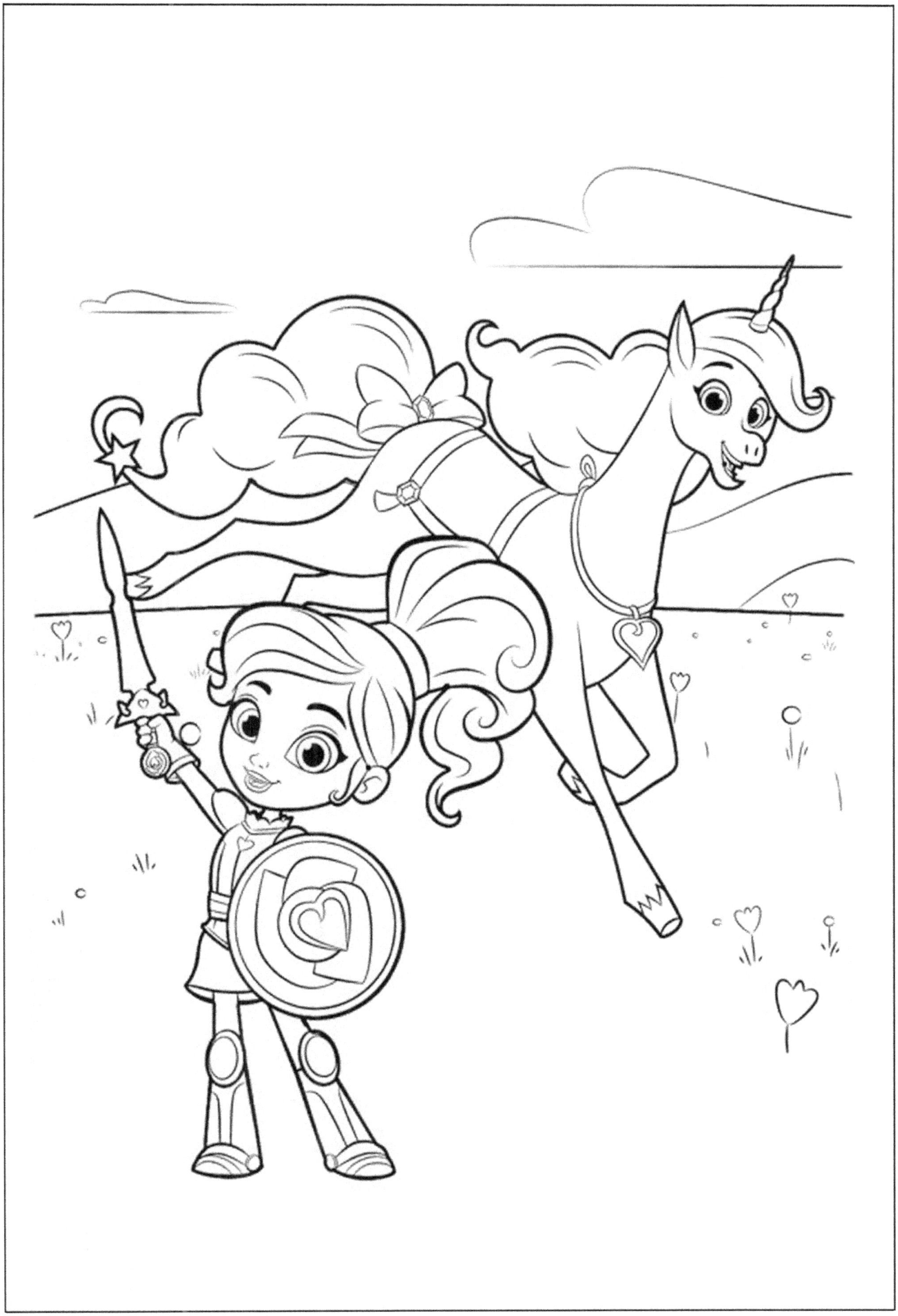

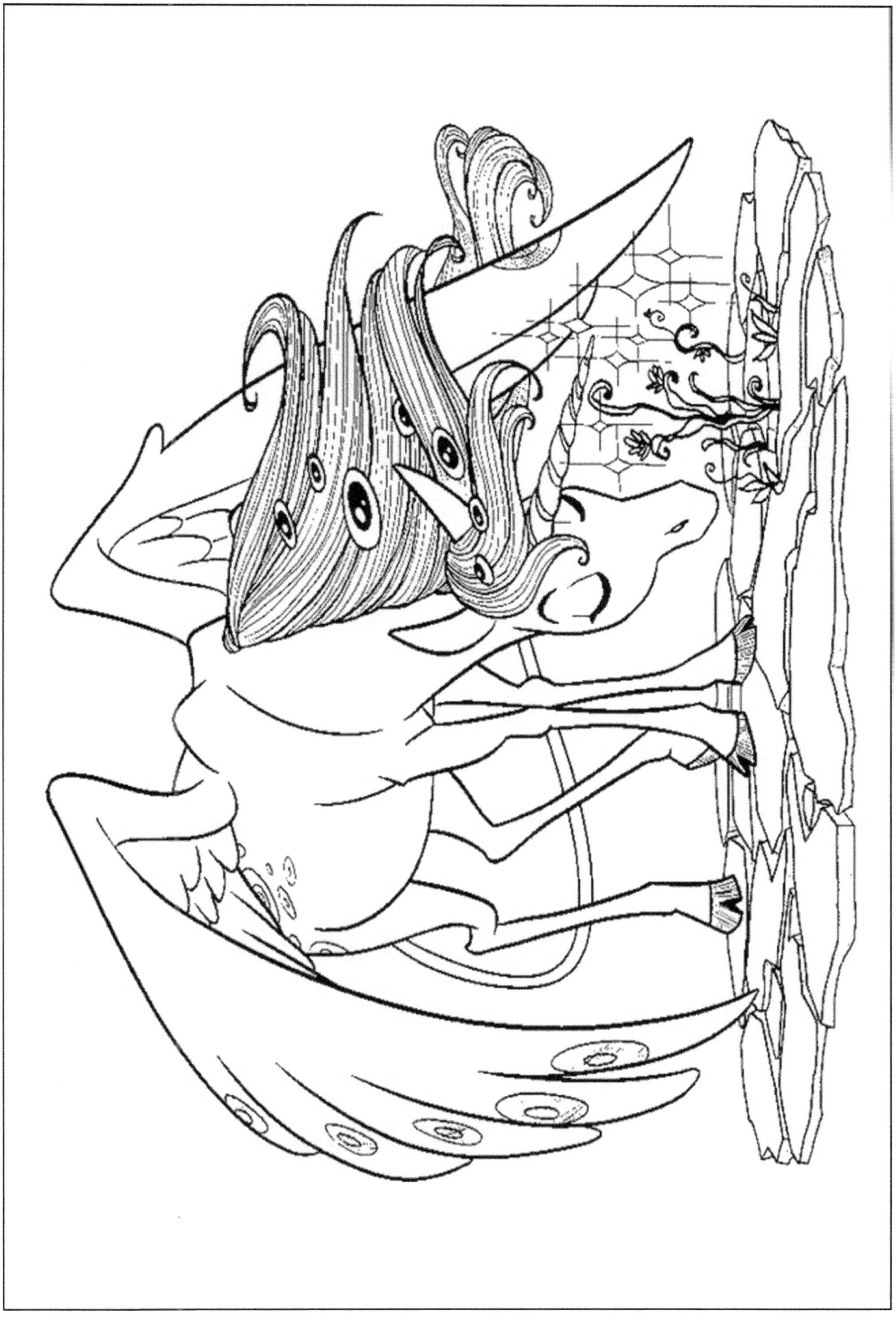

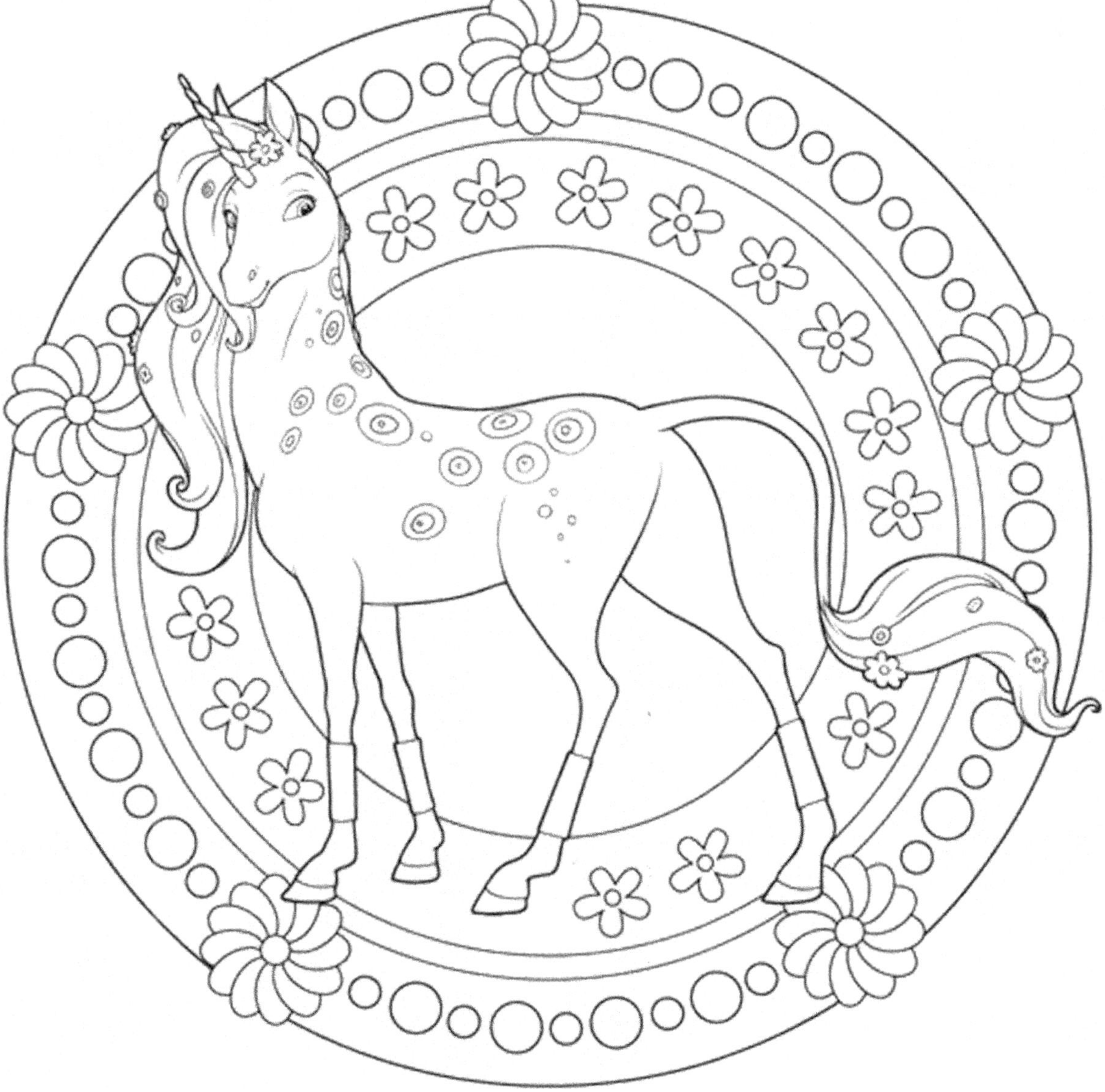

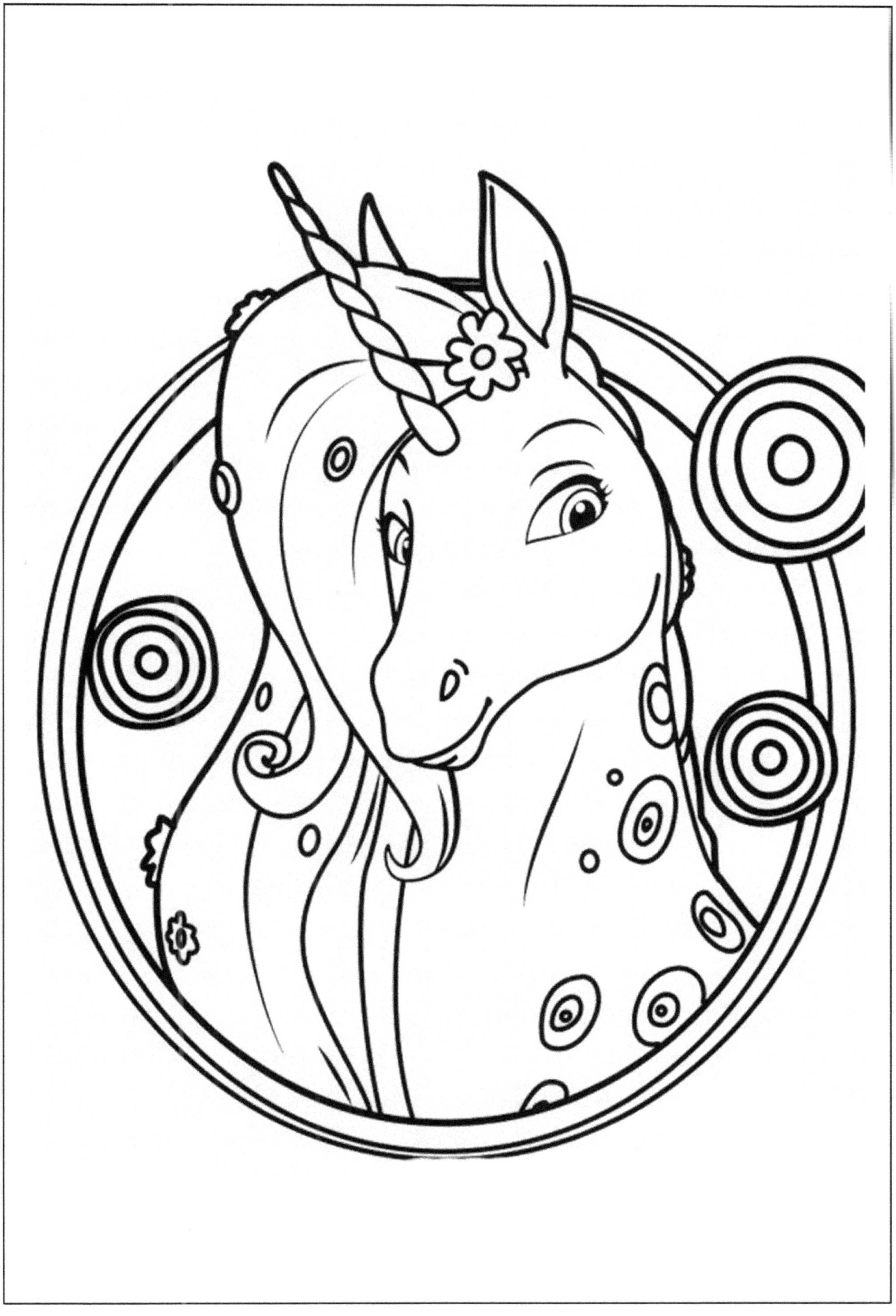

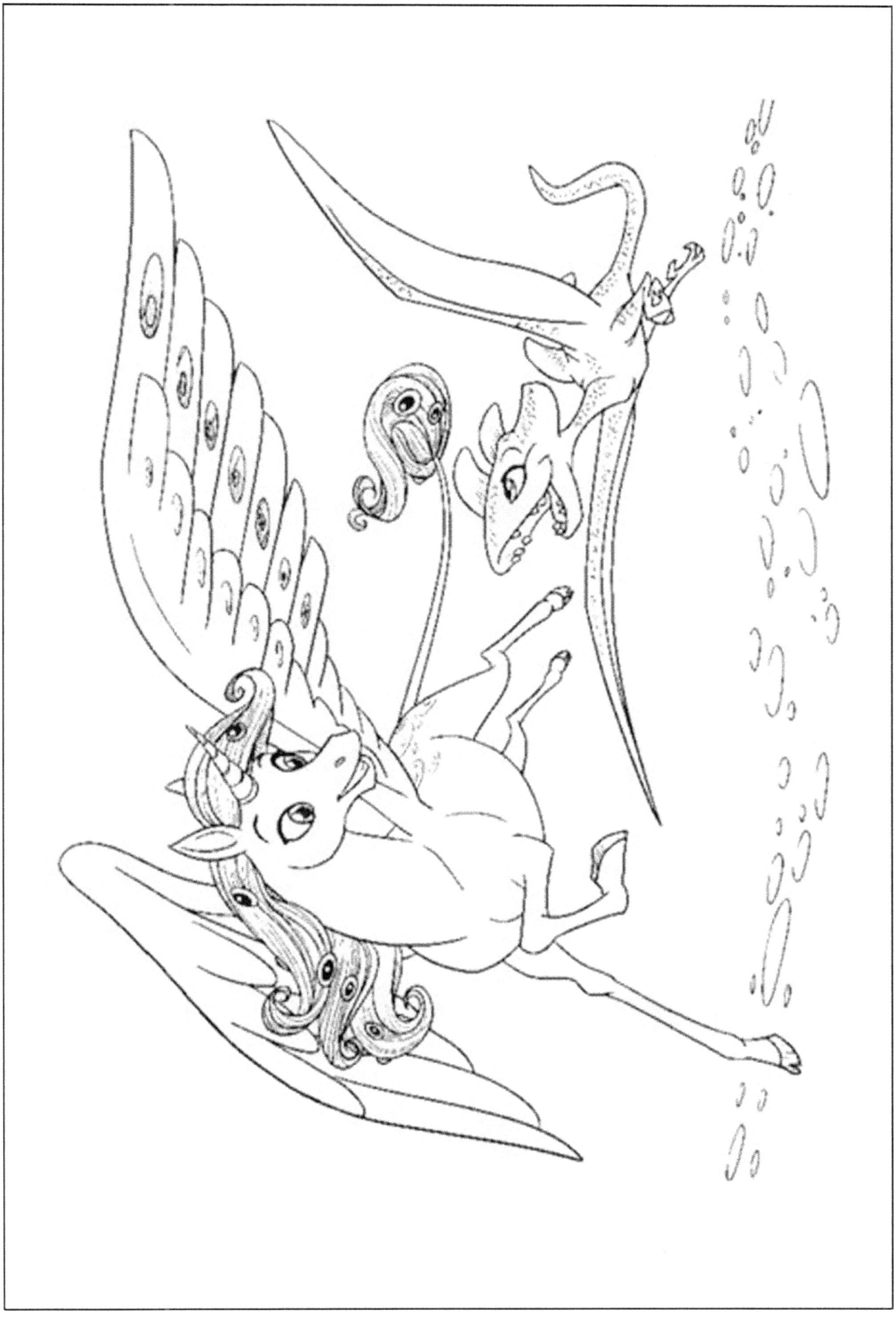

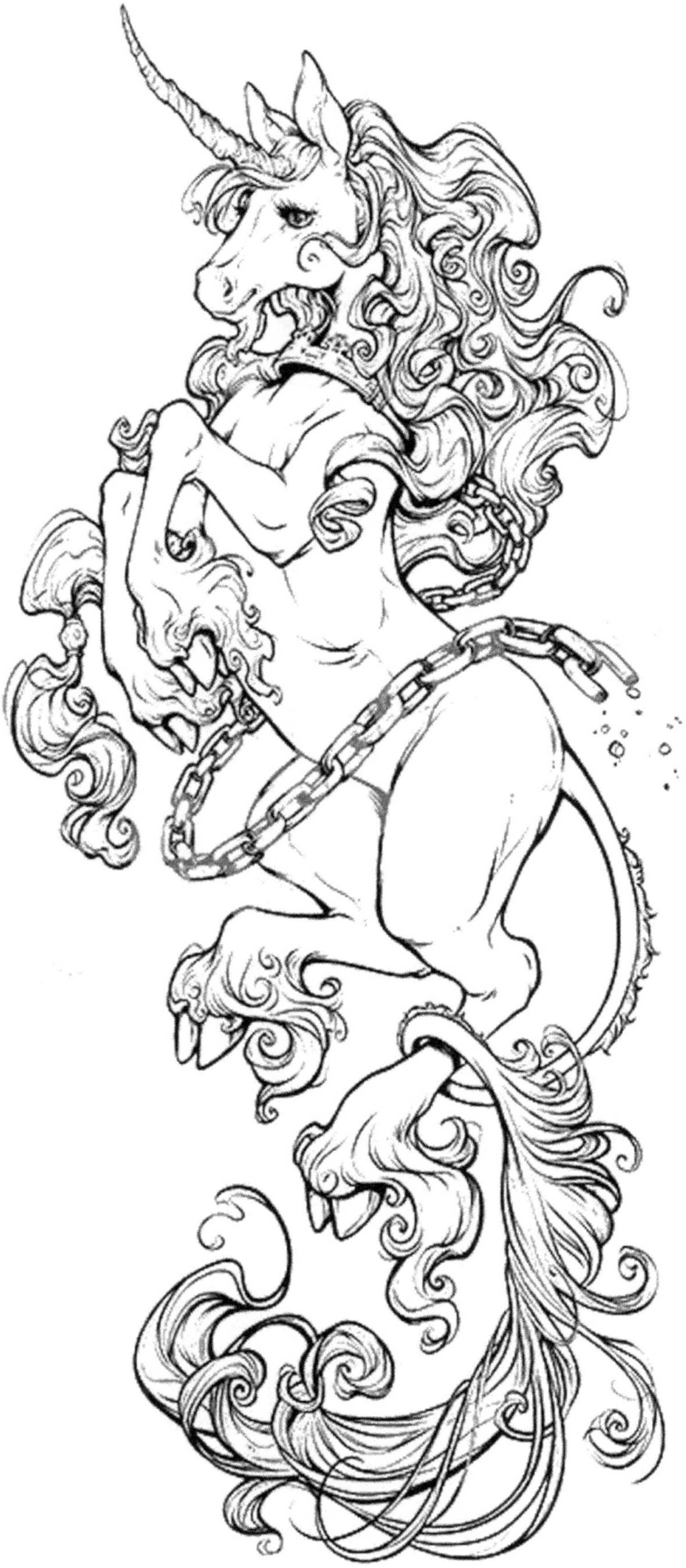

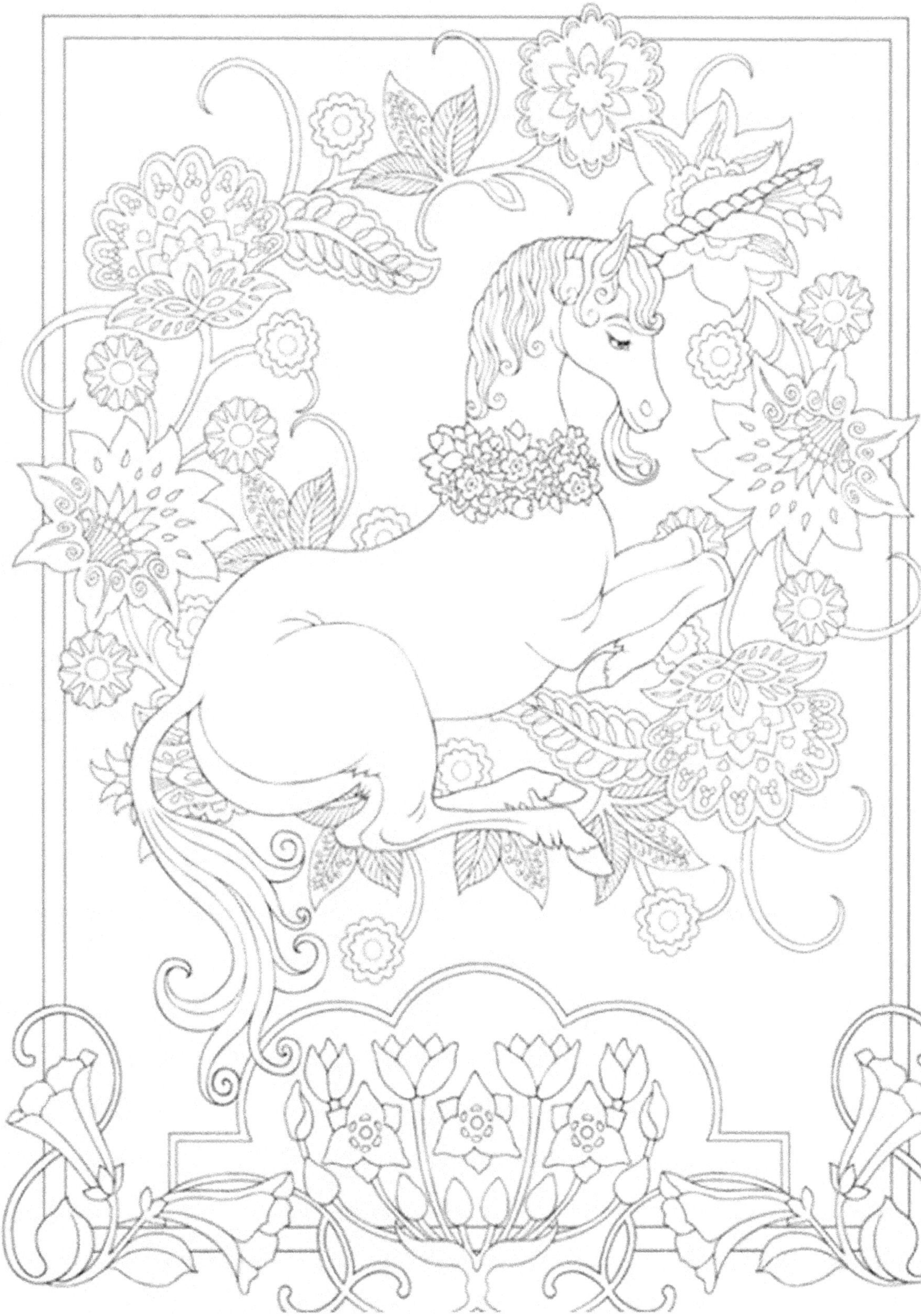

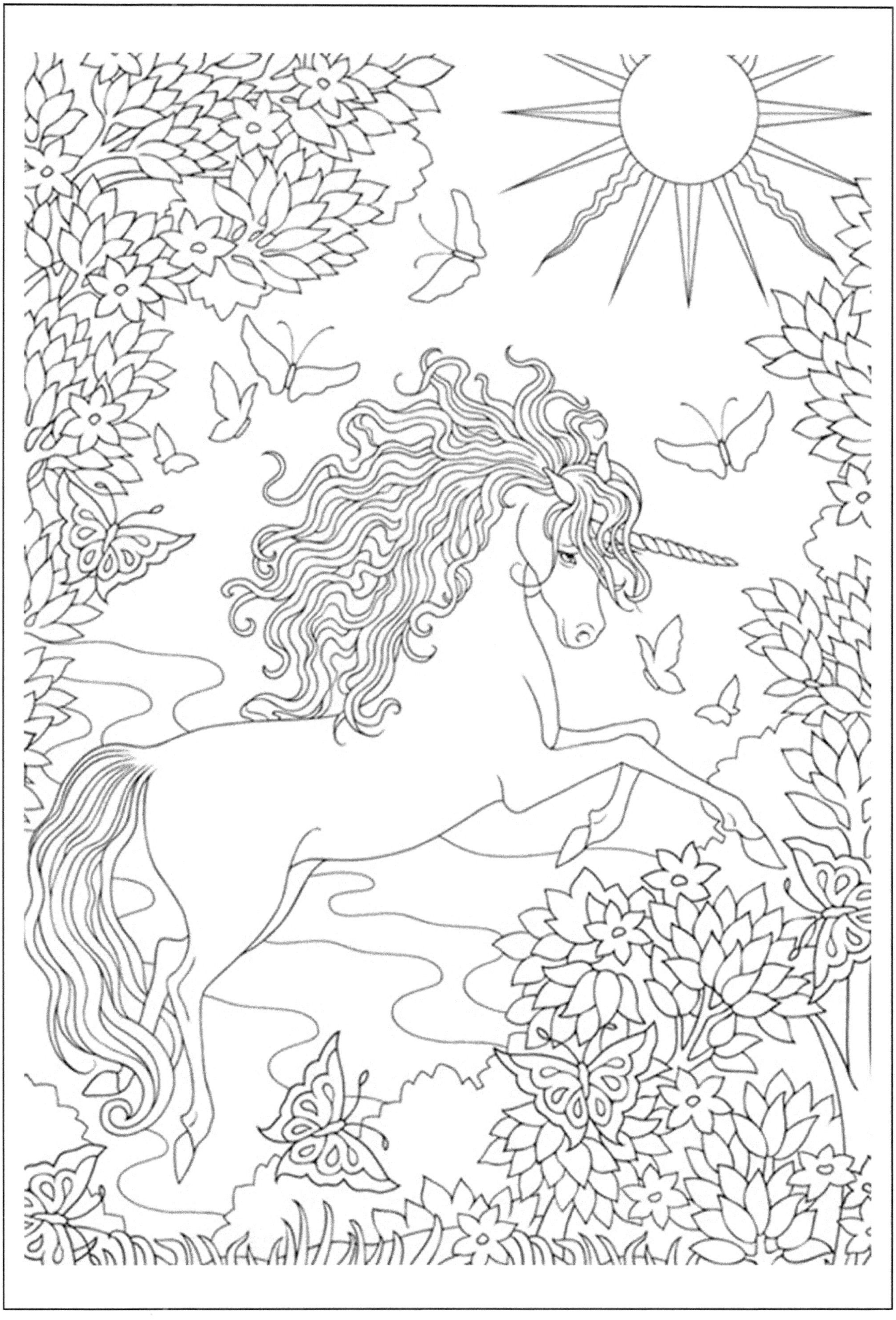

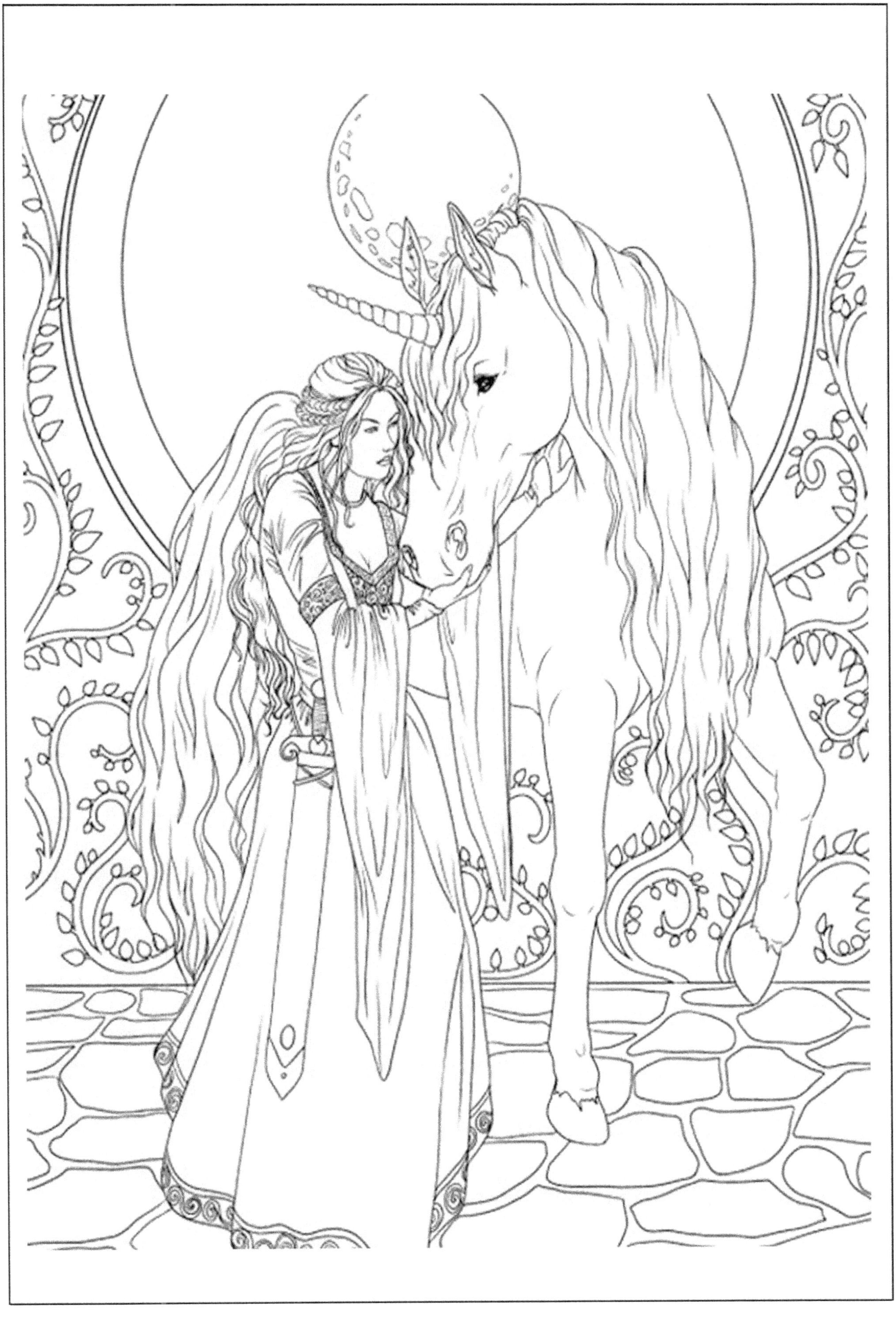

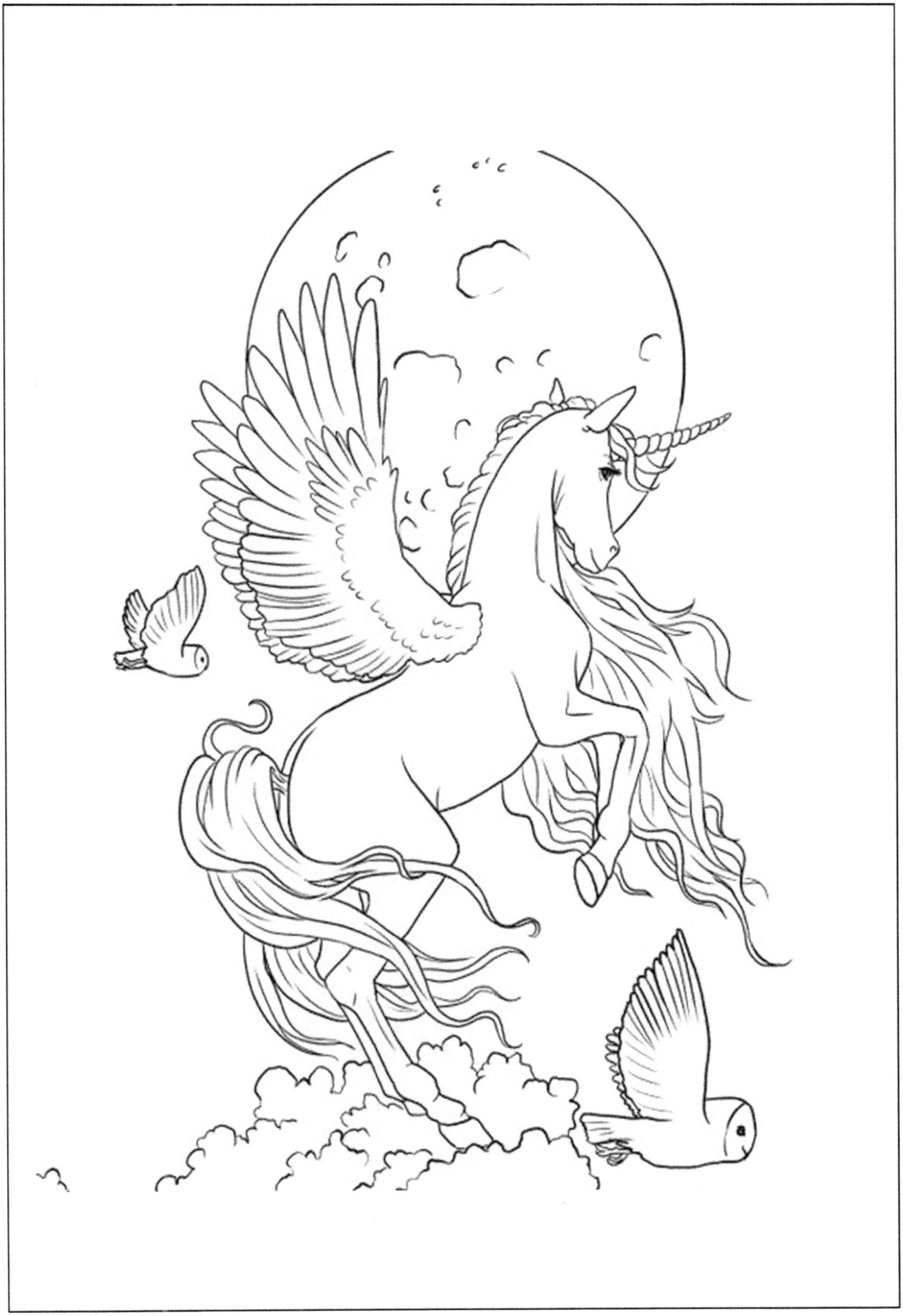

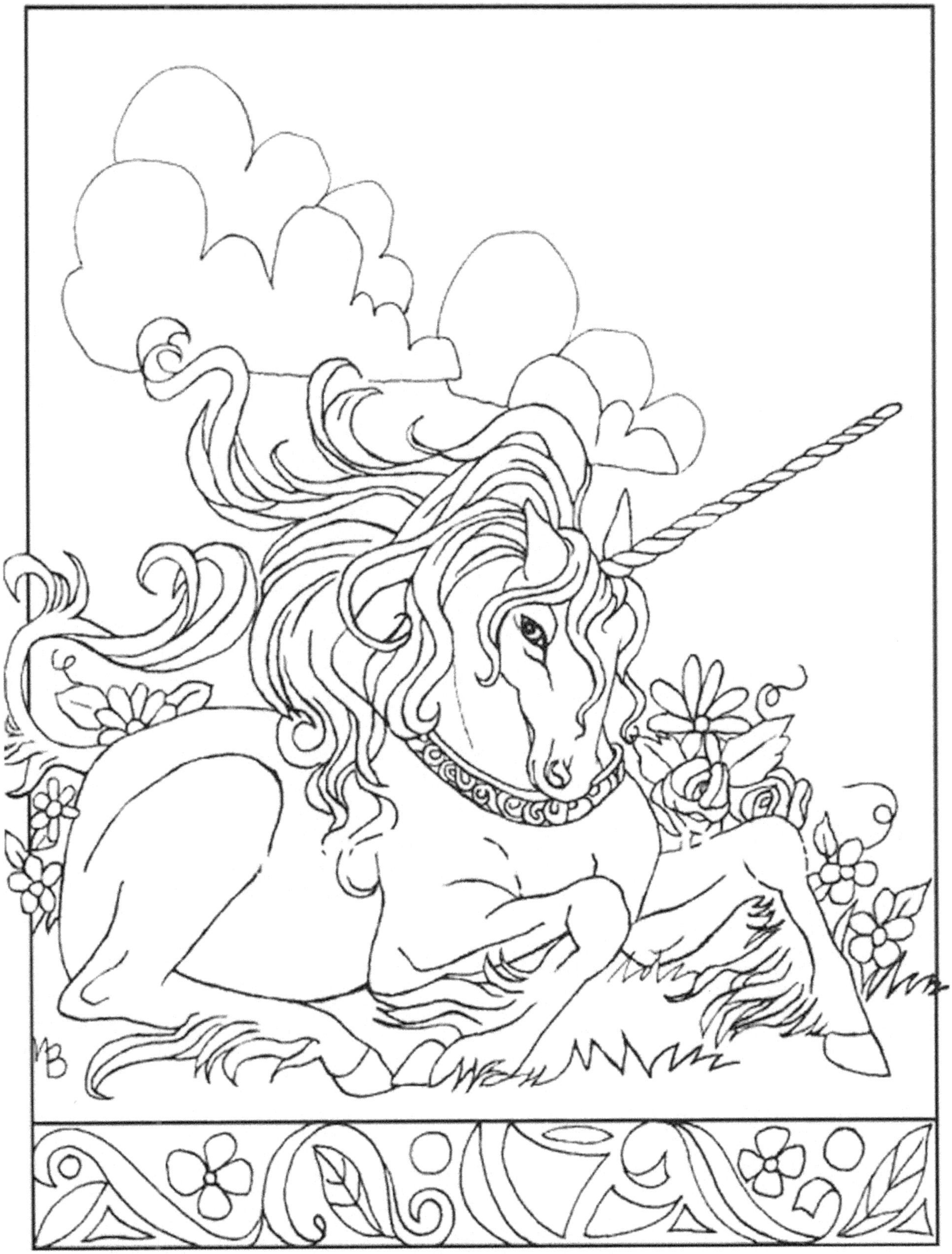

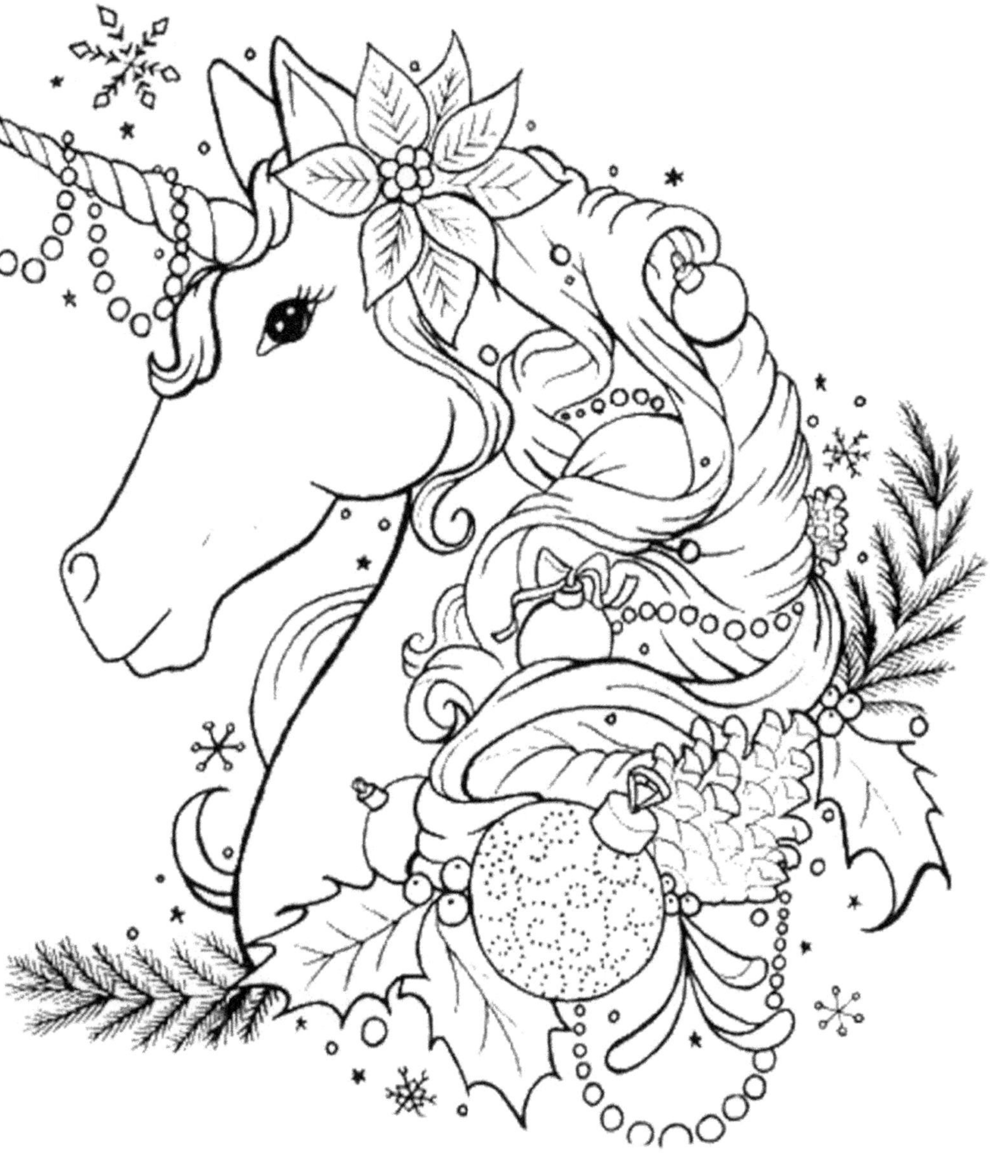

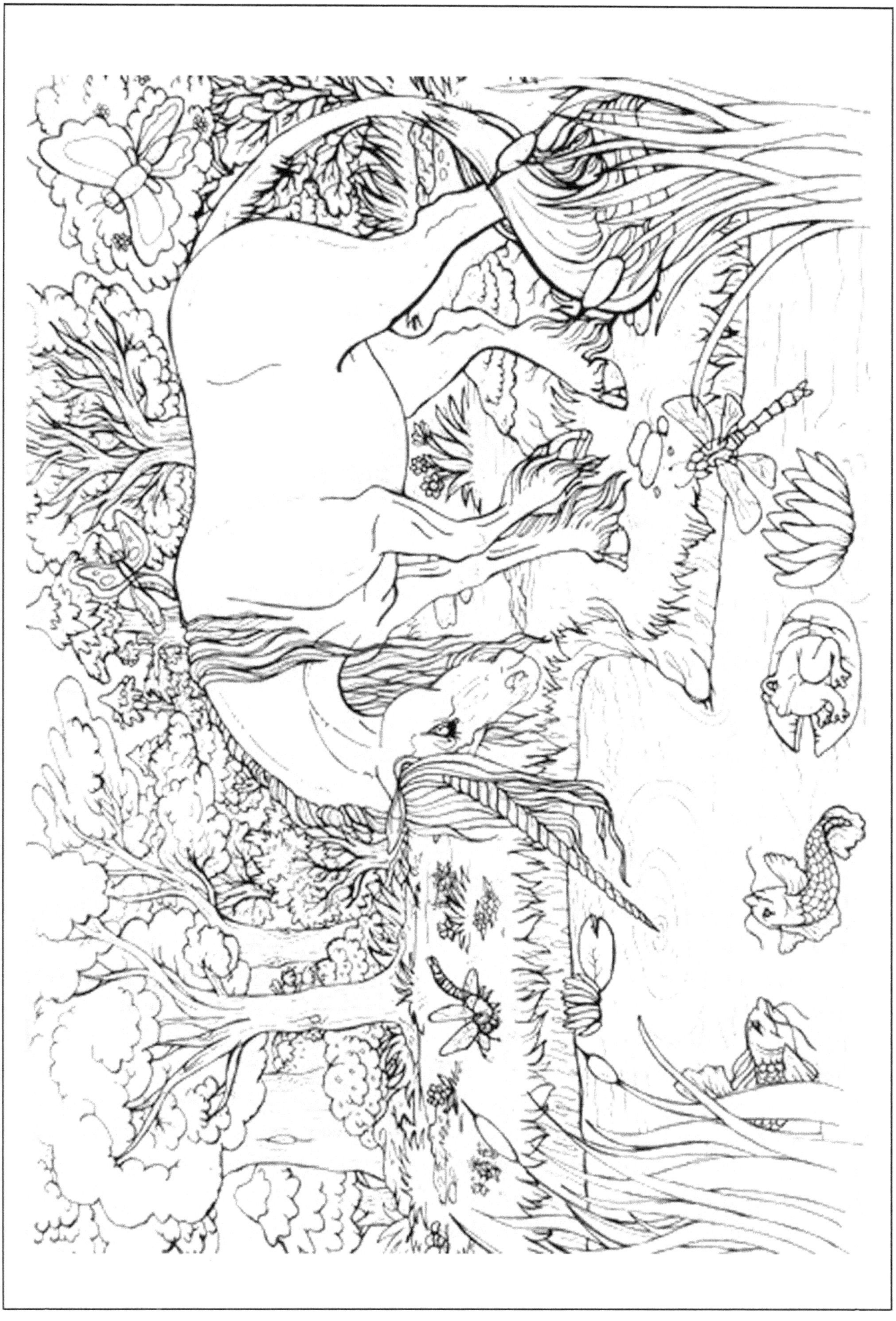

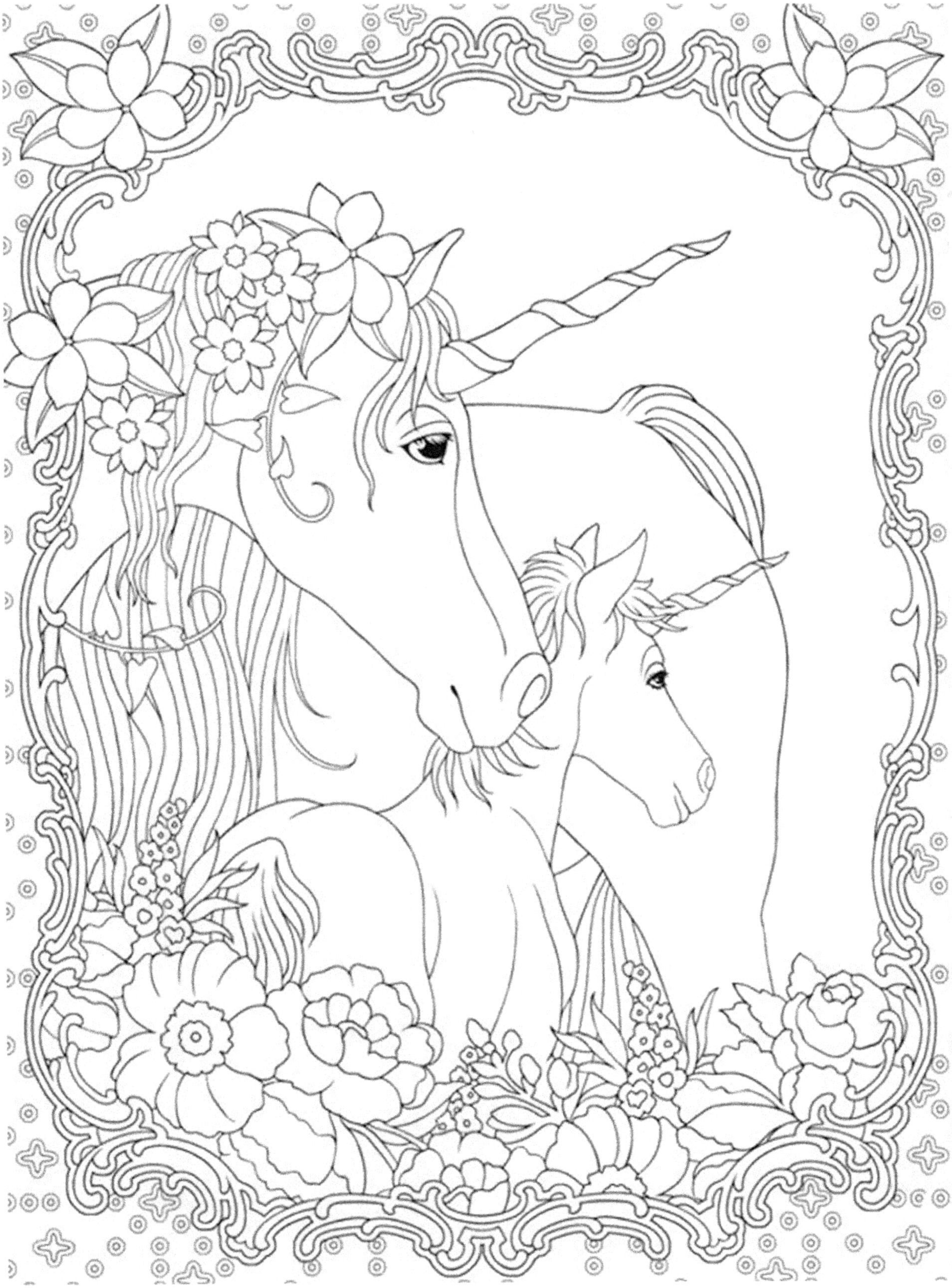

www.ingramcontent.com/pod-product-compliance
Lightning Source LLC
Chambersburg PA
CBHW080030210125
20636CB00031B/589
* 9 7 9 8 6 4 0 8 6 8 6 0 9 *